Book of One :-)
Volume 5
Group Consciousness Messages

SAM

Copyright © 2020 SAM

ISBN 978-1-939890-24-5

All rights reserved.

Brief quotations embodied in critical articles and reviews allowed. Include the book's title, author's name, and the SAM I AM PROductions website (SamIAMproductions.com) as sources of further information. Contact the author via the above website to comment, for written permission regarding longer excerpts, or to otherwise use or reproduce this book.

Views expressed in this book are solely those of the author's perception at the time of writing. Channeled material flowed through the author from October 2018 through April 2020. The author makes no warranties as to the accuracy, completeness, timeliness, or usefulness of this information. The author's intent is only to share information to help you in your quest for emotional and spiritual well-being. You are solely responsible if you use any of the information in this book for any purpose.

Because of the dynamic nature of the Internet, Web addresses or links contained in this book may have changed since publication and may no longer be valid.

This book is dedicated to all aspects of all that is, was and ever will be. It is an honor to now merge and return to Oneness after experiencing, expressing, balancing and determining what we are not.

Contents

Author's Note	xiii
Alphabetical Listing Of Messages	1
A	
A Galactic Federation of Light Message	3
B	
Building Your Future	4
C	
Change Timelines Using Emotion And Thought	5
Changing Holographic Reality Foundations	7
Choices: Duality/Separation, Oneness/Power	9
Clearing Detriments To Safety And Survival	10
Courses Of Action	12
Crystalline And Lifestyle Changes	15
D	
Dimensional Realms	17
E	
Ecstasy And Agony	18
F	

	Fears, Worries and Latent Abilities	20
	First Stage Of Awakening	21
	Further Expression Upon Applying Freedom Codes	22
G		
	Grand Mal Seizure Ploys	24
	Great Central Sun Energies	25
I		
	I AM Presence Message	26
	Incorporating Higher Self	27
	Incorporating Ones Monad	28
M		
	Merging Higher Self With Physicality	30
	Mirrors, Misthoughts And Oneness	31
	Morphing Physicality And Mass Human Death	32
N		
	Non-Local Reality Guidelines	34
O		
	Old Thought Forms Challenging New Earth	35
P		
	Pay Attention To Your Mirrors	38

R	
Recognizing Oneness Through Chaos	40
S	
Soul Whispers	42
Soul's Choices	44
Souls Leading The Way	45
Souls Playing Games	46
Spreading The Light Of Truth	48
Stay In Your Own Field Of Consciousness	49
T	
Tapping Into Greater States Of Awareness	50
Tapping Into One's Soul Plan	52
The Consciousness Of Oneness Lies Inside	53
Through Chaos Comes Remembering	55
Timeline Jumps	57
Trees of Faith	58
W	
Whispers Of Soul Self	59
Wisdom And Consciousness	60

Part Two: Author's Experiences	63
B	
Becoming More In BEingness	65
C	
Changing Human Experience	67
Chaos' Purpose	69
Consider The Law Of One During Interactions	71
D	
Departed Daughter's Message	73
Different States Of Consciousness	75
Dimensions Of Consciousness	78
E	
Ego Acting Out Separation As Family Chaos	81
F	
Forming Group Consciousnesses	84
From There To Here	86
Fruits Ripen From Past Labors	96
G	
Goddess Of Wisdom	98
Gold Comes After Listening	100

H		
	Heart Opening	102
M		
	Moving Into Christ Consciousness	104
	Multi-Generational Beliefs	106
P		
	Phases Of Chaos	108
	Physicality's Game Changes, Yet Again	111
S		
	Stay Clear In Your Intention	112
	Storm Originations, Destinations, Love And Light	114
T		
	Thought Forms Guide Human Experience	116
V		
	Vestiges of Old World Aspects Devolve	120
W		
	Wag The Dog: Infectious Influence	122
	Wayshowers, Come Forth	124
Y		
	Yonder Classes	126
Z		
	Zoning Into 5D Consciousness	128

Source Listing

A

A Mass Of Consciousness That Has Not Experienced Life In Human Form Nor As Souls
78

Aspects of My Higher Self
50,81,100,106,114

C

Conglomeration Of Higher Realm Aspects
40

G

Galactic Federation of Light
3,46,108

Goddess Of Wisdom
98

Group Consciousness Of Aspects Of *All That Is*
65

H

Higher Realms Of Consciousness
10

Higher Self
27

I

I AM Presence
26

L

Lemurian Council of Twelve
15,21,22,30,31,34,38,45,48,71,96,116

P

Pleiadian Council of Twelve
25

Pleiadians (Of Higher Bands Of Consciousness)

	57
S	
SAM	32,52,67,84,86,111,122,126,128
Sisters and Brothers of Light	7,18,60
Soul Self	59
W	
White Winged Consciousness of Nine	5,9,12,17,20,24,28,35,42,44,49,53,55,58,69,75, 102,104,112,120,124
WOW	73
About the Author	130
Index	131

Author's Note

Throughout the years, many wonderful and unexplained experiences have led me to the conclusion that this world and everything in it are thought forms meant to help us awaken to the one true state of BEing. This world is our soul's playground to experience, express and eventually come into balance not only in the mind/body/spirit system but all aspects of consciousness, universes which lie within each seemingly separate human. Details on my beliefs about our origin, why we're here, and our purpose, are clearly noted in *Book of One Volume 1*. It's in the Preface of that volume and freely online as part of the book sample.

Within this earth game and beyond there are an infinite number of veils and levels, if you will, of consciousness. Upon reaching each one, as in a video game, we move on to the next level and it is often with the assistance of what appears as unseen energies that we progress. Each dimension holds clues to our awakening but no single dimension holds all clues or answers. Only though direct experience may we be able to briefly relish in what some refer to as "Clear Light." I trust experience will, at some point in time, take you there.

SAM
Spring 2020
Fort Lauderdale, Florida

Part One

~

Book of One :-)

Volume 5

Group Consciousness Messages

A Galactic Federation of Light Message

"The Galactic Federation of Light wishes all to know the niceties you see will disappear in coming months (getting the impression the so-called new virus is designed to change the world on a global scale). As this time/space continuum continues to change and morph, the crystalline substances of those ready to morph with earth change as well.

"Yet there are those not willing to forgo these changes. The personas of those not willing to forgo these changes will continue to move to what many refer to as the 'dark side.' Those experiencing the darker aspects of the small self, of the little mind, will experience a cleansing, a purging unlike any other in your time/space continuum. Those experiencing the crystalline changes within the form in the small mind will forgo these negative aspects to experience the lighter aspects within your time/space continuum. The lighter aspects within your time/space continuum are those of greater unity with earth and all upon her.

"This duality will continue for quite some time on your earth. We, The Galactic Federation of Light are available to assist those wishing to nurture the sense of Oneness."

Building Your Future

"The seeds of tomorrow are planted today. Each emotion, each thought carries a certain charge. And the charge you give to that emotion and thought builds what you call your future."

Change Timelines Using Emotion And Thought

"Move on in your state of awareness. As you know, your focus determines your awareness. In other words, what you choose to focus on in your mind and emotions becomes more solid in your world. Many of those seeming physical forms outside what seems as your form are here to play the continuing game of separation, and in this timeline the experience shall be quite different than in the experience of those few desiring to experience greater aspects of the Self.

"Each soul chose upon coming into form to awaken at varied states of consciousness and to sense the greater aspects of human life in new ways. But the time is here for all to choose again, for humanity has gifted itself with the choice to again chose its experience using the five and now sixth sense detected by those willing to experience more open avenues of the human mind.

"As humanity moves into this great awakening more fully, it shall become strikingly apparent, the timelines cross one another with each emotion, which carries the human form to yet another experience. We do not wish to alarm you, but it is vital to now monitor emotion and thought as some who play the game, from more conscious aspects, which some humans may know as seedy or even evil, again manipulate the unknowing masses to meet and further their own agendas of greed and control.

"As many move though this process of life, determining their path and timeline with emotions and thoughts, we again ask: 'What do you choose when faced with fearful conditions?'

"This alone will lead one to another space of time in the timeline of humanity. Those choosing fear will be faced with fear after fear until they leave the planet or choose the choice of love, for it is nigh time to end the game of duality where one may be controlled by another through power and greed.

"We are the White Winged Consciousness of Nine and we are here as a group of souls, having been in human form at other times in what appears to be humanity's spectrum of linear events, to assist those ready to awaken to the truth of Oneness and Love."

Changing Holographic Reality Foundations

"Foundations and holding require the belief in ones self to create massive change, not only within ones self, but within the world of linear reality. Foundations of holding require one with great faith to know that the time/space continuum in human life is not as it appears and is malleable. This holographic reality can be changed to ones liking. This is occurring now as more humans come forth to share the Light of One, to share the Light of Oneness, co-creating the world they wish to live in. The chaotic aspects of the world are increasing to a point where all will come onboard to make these changes of Positivity, Love and Light.

"We of higher realms wish all to know, the assistance one requires is merely a thought away. Imagination is the key to be brought into the non-local reality where all becomes known. Your changes are already made for it is the world of Present Moment possibilities already existing in parallel realities. Know that as humanity moves forth on the scale of evolution, those not bearing, not sharing the Light of One, those not believing in life-affirming aspects of consciousness, now quickly dissipate back into the Void only to once again enter in form or formless states to clear misthoughts of consciousness.

"All are guided; few listen. Know that as these days darken on your earth it is merely a matter of tapping into the guidance that is already there, taking the time to listen to make those changes necessary to live a life-affirming consciousness for all of humanity.

"We your Sisters and Brothers of Light know this Oneness has already occurred, has never left and is now becoming fully recognized by many on earth. Oneness is merely a thought away and this knowing is held by more upon the earth than in any time in your history, illusion that it is. Clear space within your cluttered world and mind to make room for this knowing of Oneness and Love.

"And so it is we leave you now with the knowing of the truth of Oneness that exists within all space, all time, every aspect of BEing."

Choices: Duality/Separation, Oneness/Power

"We, the White Winged Consciousness of Nine are here to report. All upon your earth now changes as energies from unseen realms take greater hold within and upon your earth. The days of separation are ending but not until they have reached their furthest point in your spectrum of duality. Prepare for the days ahead when all shall be pushed into separation, if they choose to do so. Know, as celestial beings in essence, there is no separation and it is only in your earth world that this exists to assure that all aspects of *All That Is* see themselves within the eyes of another. The only way to Oneness again for all is to be in separation long enough to hold compassion for another human within your own body/mind system. These days will be afforded much assistance from unseen realms but it is those humans who hold the Light of One, the Oneness of which you truly are and now recognize, that will make the most change on your earth. Remember, all thought, all emotion, all words make a difference in the illusion of your world. And those that go forth to share the Light of One are now enabling many more to recognize the Oneness within themselves and humanity.

"We leave you now with this thought: You are the Truth you came to seek on earth and it is only through your understanding of the POWER you hold within that earth shall return to its rightful and original aspect of One."

Clearing Detriments To Safety And Survival

"Purging aspects of one's lower self is easier when not mired down in the chaos of every day life. This is a well-known fact among the elite that now move forward with plans to destroy all aspects of Higher Self through chaos and confusion. This does not mean that one need concentrate on these lower aspects of life, but instead take care to avoid falling into the chaos and confusion that now fills earth.

"It is with the greatest love and care, that Higher Realms Of Consciousness now assist humanity by acknowledging, there is but one true state of BEing, that of formless, non-density, which exists merely to BE, to exist in a state of wonder and awe filled with Oneness. Many on earth have forgotten this state, while seeming to exist on earth in survival mode, a state of utter confusion and loss.

"By tapping into the True State of BEing, through silent contemplation, meditation and stillness, one more easily connects with the higher aspects of Self. Only a glimmer of this state is required to open one up to the truth of formlessness, a formless consciousness that fills earth with a seamless flow of Oneness.

"The days ahead shall continue to fill with emotions, thoughts and physical experiences of separation for all who consider this earth a place of chaos and separation. But for ones that seek the wisdom of Self, that BEing of formless oneness and light within the heart's core, there shall be clear thinking and action toward a Nirvana seldom remembered without tapping into stillness.

"Aside from the consciousness of ones mind, body system there exists a true Reality, never separated. Willingness to reach this state of being will clear the chaos and confusion and allow one to physically clear all detriments to safety and survival."

Courses Of Action

"Seeming to possess a mind within a body on earth, one may follow logical trains of thought to proceed to what seems as logical conclusions. One can also tune into ones essence and follow the heart consciousness to conclude completely different thoughts. So what avenue does one take to secure the best life?

"Obviously the train of thought and heart resonance that one has focused on for aeons no longer works if one believes they are a soul in human form experiencing life after life in a game on earth.

"Does believing all is illusion work to help one through the maze to avoid chaos, which seems to be increasing on earth?

"Following ones own source of truth can easily lead one to the logical and heart based conclusion that all is indeed illusion.

"But before one achieves this great feat of evolved consciousness, all thought forms and energetic strings holding the consciousness to earth, the so-called illusory soul, must be dissipated. This occurs as one continues to address all thoughts as illusion, while seeming to balance the experience of soul on the earth plane. For as time seems to continue in a space referred to as earth, it is only through moving through the matrix of illusion that one can free itself from energetic thought forms.

"Yes, the Law of Attraction does play into each human's life and chaos appears or seems to appear as time seems to unfold, but it is merely a matter of moving through the chaos as an experience rather than a trial that assists one in achieving the end result of freedom from all energetic thought forms. In other words, what we resist persists. What we allow to unfold in its own manner, moving through it without reaction but conscious response achieves the feat of freedom in the sense that experience balances and thought, having been allowed to unfold in its own manner, dissipates without resistance.

"Shall we approach this in another way? While seeming to live on earth in human form one moves through the process from infant to adult. During this evolving consciousness, the thought form of a human evolves to a point where it no longer wishes to experience life in form (having connected with the energetic thought form of a soul taking on life after life). This is not to say that all humans are ready to end their stints in experience and expression on earth but to merely note that many seeming to be on earth at this time are ready to return to the Source of all things, or experience and express in different ways.

"As confusing as this may seem, it is of note that each human awakens to its Essence in its own time. The unwillingness to awaken to illusion is a valid choice for those who choose it. And yet the game continues as long as individual aspects of Creation experience what seems as life on earth.

"Aspects of consciousness now gather as One, remembering the unity of all things to play games in other areas of consciousness. But it is only through the total dissipation of all energetic thought forms that one achieves this feat.

"So how does one go about achieving this feat of dissipating energetic thought forms? By continuing to move though the process of evolution, responding as necessary when faced with situations appearing via the Law of Attraction. Seeking to engage in energetic thought forms serves only to increase their value, making them appear more 'real' in the world. But again, by allowing the flow of life expression and experience to show one where they are on the path of evolution and facing each circumstance with response, as needed, rather than reaction, serves one best."

White Winged Consciousness of Nine

Crystalline And Lifestyle Changes

"Downloads continue for those able to withstand these energies. We are the Lemurian Council of Twelve here to report. This cycle in your Ascension Process is nearly complete; it shall end in mid-May (2019 – and yet cycles shall continue until the end of this Golden Age).

"As each human body coalesces with these energies, the body undergoes crystalline changes within. These changes cause the body to function at a higher vibrational level. Changes also affect the body in what may appear as detrimental ways as the clearing and cleansing of Self continues. It is vital at this time to maintain health in all aspects, resting as desired (especially when the body suddenly becomes exhausted), maintaining hydration and eating wholesome foods, for as these energies continue to enter your earth effects upon the body continue.

"Know that we are with you guiding this process, which many of you have been through many times before. Know that this is a natural process that all undergo at some appointed time within their own soul plan if they have agreed to do so. Know that as each undergoes this process, one's lifestyle continues to make vast changes. The old ways are dropping away quickly for those undergoing this process. Allow the new to enter and replace these old lifestyle ways. There may be a time of great void in many undergoing this process, a time where relationships dissolve, a time where gross disturbances in lifestyle occur, but one must maintain the attitude of being souls undergoing a process that has taken place many times on your earth, while in many forms.

"We are the Lemurian Council of Twelve and we wish you to know, the guidance is there for you to tap into at any point in your time/space continuum."

Dimensional Realms

"Many dimensional realms are available for one to tap into at will. One needs only to have the desire to do so. As these higher energies continue to bombard earth, compliments of other planets including the sun and moon, more humans will become aware of the ability to tap into other aspects of their own thought forms.

"We the White Winged Consciousness of Nine are here to assist those that wish to move further from the matrix prison humanity devised as a learning tool, to recognize that *All That Is* is truly the only aspect to dwell within. Know that as each human progresses in their experience, they will tap into higher and higher aspects of their own illusion, their own thought forms, to dissipate them and continue in thought, form and deed to the Truth of Oneness once again.

"We are the White Winged Consciousness of Nine here to assist those ready to ask."

Ecstasy And Agony

"The times before you now are a mixture of ecstasy and agony. As those moving forward into the greater timeline of humanity to one filled with Love, Light and Oneness reach the ecstasy of their True BEing, those choosing other timelines based on separation and fear face the agony.

"It is done as you believe in this world of emotion and thought. Knowing all now move quickly toward Oneness regardless of (their own) consciousness, assist those that know this True Self is arising from the ashes of wasteful eons now left behind by those choosing to relish in the Oneness of *All That Is*, bearing in mind and living the Law Of One.

"It is with the greatest respect that we, your Sisters and Brothers of Light, your Lemurian, Pleiadian, Arcturian, Syrian and all Sisters and Brothers of Light, now ask you to choose your timeline carefully. For each reaction, each choice within your daily movements chooses that timeline. It may not be a conscious choice. The timeline you find yourself in may be the choice of an unconscious reaction spurred forth through the separation humanity now moves through.

"As this chaos continues to clear on earth, be aware that all serving and living by the Law Of One shall not be faced with the chaos others seem to bear. And yet each soul, as noted many times, has made its choice (choosing the best soul plan of experience for each lifetime). Although free will exists on planet earth, many will not use their free will to change that soul choice before birth. But know that choice does exist. It is available for those that wish to choose differently than their soul has chosen to experience. We, your Sisters and Brothers of Light, now leave you in the consciousness of One, knowing that all existing upon earth at this time play a unique role in the process of returning to the Whole in all aspects."

Fears, Worries and Latent Abilities

There are often those who are misguided in thinking they tap into Source energy. We wish to offer a few tips to those moving toward this long-lost ability.

Frequency changes when tapping into higher realms. The body begins to vibrate at an advanced level, sometimes in the beginning shaking as it adjusts. With this change in frequency comes a change in temperature. The body begins to feel heat as this frequency increases. Some may not wish to withstand this change in frequency and so tap into the astral energies to avoid it.

Those wishing to tap into these higher realms, available to all, must prepare their host. Knowing that a host free of negativity makes a better channel of higher realms, we leave you with these words to ponder:

Do I wish to be a channel of higher realms?

Am I willing to let go of all I know of how the world revolves and devolves?

Am I willing to change all beliefs to recognize I am the Creator?

White Winged Consciousness of Nine

First Stage Of Awakening

"Valleys of lows and highs extend throughout the Ascension Process. We are the Lemurian Council of Twelve here to report to all this process that humanity now moves through is yet the first stage of awakening to the True Self; the second stage being that which occurs without the carbon-based form."

Further Expression Upon Applying Freedom Codes

"All will be gifted with the ability to align fuller with earth's magnetics. We the Lemurian Council of Twelve assist all who wish to align with this changing magnetic field of earth and humanity. As all of earth's magnetics continue to change, all upon her must change and align as well.

"Onslaught's of energies continue to exist within the illusory realm and yet many now know the holographic energies holding the illusory matrix together dissipates with each thought of freedom. Freedom codes were released during earth's 2019 year and all upon earth will now have the opportunity to align with earth's magnetics, assisting them in reaching greater states within the awareness of the illusion.

"Those wishing to continue to play the game of non-freedom shall leave this earth to rebirth in other illusory forms and formless astral states to continue the game until their illusory soul has reached its point of fulfillment. Those remaining on the New Earth shall continue to align with earth's magnetics.

"This process will not be as easy and graceful as one would wish.

"All will know the matrix illusion is easily left behind when one fully aligns with the higher Spirit Self, having fulfilled desires of its illusory soul, having merged all experience and expression on earth into other states of Consciousness, coalescing back for the final time into the Oneness of all that is, was and ever will be.

"*A Special Note:* It is desired by souls within the illusion living upon a New Earth to apply freedom codes to live in form as sovereign individuals before too fully aligning all experience and expression to coalesce with the Oneness of all that is, was, and ever shall be. We, the Lemurian Council of Twelve – a group of Consciousness, souls having coalesced all experience and expression as individuals – now leave this channel to create the New Earth with those wishing to align their souls' experiences and expressions into yet another seeming new group Consciousness to experience and express in higher realms of the matrix illusion. For it is only through experience and expression that all that is, was, and ever shall be senses the full expression of It's Self."

Grand Mal Seizure Ploys

"These summer months are crucial to humanity's evolution. Be aware of your propensities to continue to draw apart in separation and fear. Ploys from the lost souls of very few on your planet are being played out in the last grand mal seizure, if you will. Events on your planet that people in other areas of your United States rarely know or hear about, for lack of media attention, will continue this summer as humanity's consciousness evolves. There is nothing to stop the evolution, the awakening of humanity.

"The few who cause troublesome events are now leaving the planet en masse. Be assured that freedom in all aspects is but a short time away in your evolution as these last few ruling elite, as they like to refer to themselves, leave the planet one by one in various ways. This is not to say that those remaining will all awaken. Keep in mind that the happenings now upon your earth this summer shall never happen in the realm of humanity on earth again. We are the White Winged Consciousness of Nine and we are here to assist all as the progression of evolution continues at a rapid pace through the chaos on your earth."

Great Central Sun Energies

"The farthest reaches of your Great Central Sun are more accessible to you now as humans. In the coming days, there will be many new energies dispersed within your earth coming from the Great Central Sun. We, the Pleiadian Council of Twelve, are here to guide those ready to step up their human experience to include other planets of existence within your universe."

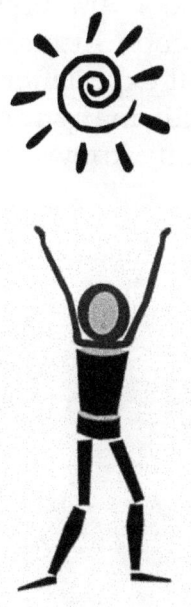

I AM Presence Message

"Invite yourself to play with these last few years of experience upon your earth. As things fall apart for many, you are rewarded with the truth and knowledge that this is not the real world of anyone's making. Know that as earth moves though these changes all upon her shall continue to experience discordant energies until they return to their True Self. Within all breeds recognition and it is humanity's goal to experience, in somewhat human form (for the human form changes as we change our DNA), recognition of the I AM Presence. Each I AM Presence within each human form desires this experience, yet all experience is unnecessary in the totality of what many refer to as God or *All That Is*. This totality knows no bounds."

Incorporating Higher Self

"As one moves through the process of incorporating Higher Self into everyday life, one needs to be aware of the vibrational rate of oneself and others as well. For moving through these coming days and months *it will be crucial to remain in ones own field of consciousness*, as all things not brought to the surface now rise to be cleared and cleansed from humanity's consciousness. Humanity now moves through what many refer to as the 'darkest of ages' but some humans have cleared enough feelings of separation to recognize that in essence all are One, now coming together in entirely new ways after seeming apart for aeons of time through humanity's experience in space and time.

"It is with the greatest respect that higher realms now watch and guide humanity through this process, even knowing on the highest level of awareness, all is in the mind of the believer."

Incorporating Ones Monad

"Within this process of accessing and processing Self, one learns to forgo the blessings of non-eternal aspects. These aspects are learned through behavioral concepts processed while in human form. All humans hold these concepts and it is during this processing and accessing True Self that these concepts are released on the physical plane, accessed, processed to no longer hold back the Monad from incorporating within the physical dimension.

"As one moves through this process of accessing, experiencing life in physicality, one is best to remain aware that all processing is of experiences within the realms of illusory thought forms. These thought forms will balance in time allowing the Self of One to incorporate within the physical form and lead one back to the trueness of ones Essence. This Essence now incorporates in many upon earth, and knowing this truth, those incorporating this Essence return in thought to Unity Consciousness, yet a small step toward the BEingness of each Essence in Reality.

"Know that as the process of returning in all aspects to the True Essence of ones Self continues on earth, the chaos surrounding the unique individual that has garnered this recognition continues to exist outside the chaos of those not holding the Unity Consciousness of ones True Self. Hold fast to the belief of Oneness and know that as this earth continues to merge back into the star planet of which it is, all is well in the small mind of one that holds not the thought of separation.

"We are the White Winged Consciousness of Nine and we are available to those wishing to tap into this aspect of Unity Consciousness."

Merging Higher Self With Physicality

"We, the Lemurian Council of Twelve, are here to report. Your earth now spins out of control for many as these new energies settle more fully. All upon your earth now know the energies are quite different than before. As your full moon arrives, it brings with it greater energies as well. Be prepared as these energies more fully coalesce upon the earth, for chaos may erupt in certain areas.

"Know that we are here to assist those ready and willing to help cement the energies of Oneness upon this New Earth. The chaos arrives to help in this effort as all move quickly toward chaos and separation or Oneness and love. There are many upon the earth assisting in this effort. If you are one, know despite your unconscious knowing, you are always guided.

"There are those among you that know they are guided and tap into this source of wisdom regularly. Take the time to tap into this wisdom. Reach out for the higher aspect of your own Self and know it is what you came to earth to achieve in this lifetime – the merging of the Higher Self with the physical body to eventually, finally, rid your Self of the need, the desire, for separation."

Mirrors, Misthoughts And Oneness

"A portal awaits for you to pass through my dear. Pay particular attention to each days' interactions with others as these mirrors present you with the final vestiges of the old to discard. These misthoughts are ready to be discarded as your mirrors bring them up, for it is your own consciousness that brings them forth. As these misthoughts are laid aside, portals open widely so that you may step through the gateways into the light of Truth and Love. Know that as you do this, many others are assisted as well. There are many of you Wayshowers that are moving through these portals to clear, cleanse and transmute these misthoughts.

"Know that as you move through this passing of time in your space as a collective, timelines shift, other portals open, other gateways merge to assist all upon planet earth, no matter the timeline nor space. It is with great pleasure that we watch as those souls ready to move forward in this what you refer to as your Ascension Process.

"Know that all is going accordingly well to the plan of the Divine One, for in your world many layers exist in returning to this Oneness. Living by the Law Of One is the next step in your progression to full sovereignty.

"We are the Lemurian Council of Twelve and we wish all to know, assistance is a mere thought away."

Morphing Physicality And Mass Human Death

From the beginning of time, life has taken on new forms in every manner of BEing. Humanity comes and goes as planetary changes, floods and so-called other catastrophes occur. As our planet gradually makes its shift back to Light, ever so slowly during these next several hundred years, scores of humans will leave the planet choosing to return to a New Earth in a new form or to continue their soul's experience on other planets.

Just as the Atlanteans, Lemurians, Mayans and others, some are now choosing to play a new game instead of extinction. Souls choosing to play this new game knew it meant leaving everything behind, to experience life on a New Earth in an entirely new form – a body with less dense carbon-based matter to one of crystalline, filled with photons that energize it as a mass of Light – able to withstand current and coming changes as humanity moves though the process with Mother Earth to be more in tune with surrounding space.

It is for this reason that today's communication comes, to alert those interested about these earth and body changes, to make all more comfortable as they occur and to cement a new thought in those with doubtful minds.

You may ask, "Am I one of those dying in physicality to leave the planet, or has my soul chosen to take on this unknown body of Light?" If you must ask, the answer should be clear.

Many souls chose to begin the process but very few chose to withstand pressures and changes to complete the cycle of returning to Light in merely one life. Those doing so are now leading the way, answering the call to alert other humans of the new game. Again, very few shall achieve the feat of morphing physicality in this lifetime, for it involves not only morphing the physical form but emotions, thoughts and memories of all lives lived on earth. Consider this as you see mass catastrophes occur throughout the world. These are meant to clear the land before it floods with the water necessary for her future cleansing.

Yes, of course, there are always other perspectives. But this particular communication addresses the issue of mass human death in a way that many humans understand, to reach out to those with greater understandings of the way consciousness works on earth, until one realizes that after all is said and done, one's life here is merely a whisper of a minute aspect of the Void that came into being through Consciousness and focused energy.

Be patient as the process of returning to Light continues for those remembering a life in Lemuria when the body was less dense for this is the new game played by those remembering their Lemurian life.

SAM

Non-Local Reality Guidelines

"Flowing through the ethers of non-space, non-local reality one must adhere to certain **guidelines**. These guidelines are easily relished by those of higher vibrational rates as humanity moves through the process of ascension. This process is not for those unable to share or gather the Light of One within themselves, but available to all who seek a greater awareness of being in human form.

"As the human condition changes to include multidimensional aspects of BEing, one must *be aware of other states of conscious awareness*. This means to **remain in the physical form living what seems as a 'normal' life, while incorporating multidimensional aspects**. Realities are different for each aspect of the Whole, each human. Yet all who seek and **live by the Law Of One** know all are one united in effort, purpose and BEing. Let those **seek**ing their **Higher Self** reap the greater awareness of Wholeness and Truth.

"We are the Lemurian Council of Twelve and we are with you always."

Old Thought Forms
Challenging New Earth

"We again wish to report on the seeding of humanity and the nine events. The struggle and strife your world faces today, and in coming days, will take one on a magical journey of awareness of Self. These nine events are necessary processes to coalesce humanity back to the Oneness many now seek. This Oneness is part of the necessary form of BEing for all. Knowing that Oneness exists is yet another step towards the Truth of remembering. Knowing of the truth of Oneness brings all aspects of the Whole of One together in spiritual awareness, together in conscious awareness as all relate to the confusion and chaos of what seems to be another.

"We the White Winged Consciousness of Nine are here to assist humanity out of this realm of separating thought forms. These thought forms have served their purpose to enrich the experience of each aspect of the Whole of One wishing to experience a journey seeming to consist of separation. The journey is not quite ended in your vernacular. It will continue for hundreds of years. Yes, we know that may seem quite arduous to many humans but please recall, as a human form those currently in human form will not recognize the fruition of this grand event in their current thought form. Recall, all within your earth is a thought form and these thought forms were seeded along with the seeding of the earth. As your New Earth continues to cement and enrich itself, these thought forms must be dissipated with the other so-called negative thought forms that built and held the earth of old, for humanity will not carry these energetic thought forms into the New Earth.

"Be aware many humans now in form will never consciously or unconsciously enter your New Earth. Know that those holding the energetic thought form of Oneness are now on this New 5D Earth. As this earth continues to evolve and enrich itself, all those upon her shall do the same. Know that in coming months the chaos and turmoil within what seems to be your New Earth is really the vestiges of the thought forms of the old earth trying to take hold. It is important to dissipate these thought forms, to no longer carry these thought forms, for your New 5D Earth will not support them. Those persisting in relishing in the energies of these thought forms of separation will continue to leave your world. Those continuing to relish in the separation of humanity are not recognizing that each thought form within their own physical mind, own physical awareness, is really an aspect of their self, waiting to be cleared. This is an important part for all of humanity to pay attention to; the thought forms are in your mind. The thought forms will continue but only with your constant thoughts of their awareness. Once you lay aside the thought forms of separation, the thought forms of Oneness cement within your vernacular and all becomes One in Truth, in Love, in Light.

"This is yet another step towards your ethereal non-form. We bid you adieu knowing that all those who chose to enter and exist within the 5D Earth will do so successfully. Those souls choosing to remain in the separation, feeding the thought forms not in conjunction with Oneness will leave this physical realm."

Pay Attention To Your Mirrors

"As the frequency and vibrational state within consciousness continues to change at an alarming rate, one may desire to be aware of their own frequency and vibration. For it is only through knowing oneself that one may continue to gauge the changes around it. Each being of consciousness is enclosed in its own field of conscious awareness and yet all are part of the Whole of BEingness. This will never change but the aspects of the Whole, the particles if you will, continue to become aware of that BEingness as all move through the time/space continuum.

"Those on earth now quickly move through the chaos of separation, through this portal of awareness. And yet, as this occurrence continues to build momentum, all humans begin to see very clearly that there are no lost particles, there are no humans on earth that are unaffected nor are there any that remain alone within their single consciousness. For as these massive changes occur on earth all coalesce within the etheric realm of consciousness, opening yet another door for those unaware of this aspect of Wholeness.

"In the coming days and months, many shall leave earth due to various dis-ease within themself. This is not necessarily a 'bad' occurrence but a joyous one as new opportunities arise for those that leave earth. These opportunities now include those that were curiously left behind by many souls that chose to not experience other aspects of Wholeness on other planets and in other states, forms or formless consciousness.

"It is with the greatest respect that we the Lemurian Council of Twelve ask all to pay attention to their own state of consciousness, their own aspect of awareness, for this is the charge of each human now upon the earth. Mirrors continue to present all with the information needed to progress beyond the illusion of separation to that of the Oneness of which all are.

"We leave you now with this thought: will each aspect continue to be separation in your mind or will you embrace those aspects of your self long forgotten?"

Recognizing Oneness Through Chaos

"Higher Self messages continue for those who wish to receive them. Speak not of your brother in haste nor tarry in the world of separation. The world now returns to the Oneness in which humanity in other realms cherished for aeons of time. As your world comes to a screeching halt in 2020, higher realms support efforts of those striving toward Oneness, striving toward unity and love of all.

"Knowing it is not an easy task to dwell in duality immersed in the grace and ease of Oneness, while many continue to swim in the sea of separation, we of higher realms support all efforts to insure the purity and wholeness of Truth in all aspects of the world. Each single aspect, institution, shall now be examined under the microscope of purity and truth. Each belief shall be secured in new ways to insure the Oneness of all. As each belief changes the reality of those on earth, bear in mind the chaos that ensures shall not last for long.

"Keep in mind, the Oneness those seek is already held within many, for it has never been left in the higher realms, and the higher realms are where many now dwell even while in physical form. We leave you now knowing the truth of Oneness held inside each aspect, each human on earth.

"We are a Conglomeration Of Higher Realm Aspects assisting humanity within ones self; 'within ones self' means each who channels, who listens to the inner core BEing of its very own mind/body/spirit complex.

"Namaste."

Soul Whispers

"In this time of earth's great distortion, there are many habits to change, if you will pardon the expression. We, the White Winged Consciousness of Nine, are always available to help humanity make the changes necessary for ascending into a higher form of consciousness. This is not so easily done but achievable in one's lifetime if the focus is entirely upon evolution.

"Hence, one sees the issue with ascension, for not many humans choose to set habits aside let alone take the time to focus solely on evolution. As the days progress, there will be many prompts to change habits. There will also be many issues and conditions to stop one from choosing evolution, for there are those not ready to end the earth game.

"Yes, we have spoke of this before but it bears a new mention, for many things in your world are coming to a head as the forces of what many refer to as good and evil compete for one's attention.

"Let your thoughts focus on the whispers of soul as the days, weeks and months ahead unfold, for this will serve the body in the best possible manner. It is not our wish to interfere with soul plans but to merely point out that each soul has chosen their plan for each life. However, humanity is now at a point where soul plans may be changed if one is dedicated to evolution as it is in the best interest of all involved that as many souls as possible ascend in consciousness to avoid undue circumstances.

"We shall leave it at that, much to the channel's dismay, not choosing to define the term 'undue' at this time. Just know, the opportunity to tap into one's soul is always there for the asking."

Soul's Choices

"Know that all is well as we move though these portals of increased consciousness. Remember, not all souls chose this increasing state of awareness so it is wise to carry your vibration within yourself and keep centered while moving though what is left of the 3D maze of consciousness.

"We are the White Winged Consciousness of Nine and we shall continue to guide all who wish to move forward into increasing states of awareness of oneself, of the universe, cosmos and ultimately, the illusion of time/space. We leave you with this thought:

"Who will you ultimately be when your journey in the body, this consciousness is complete? Will you return to play the game of illusion again or break free of the illusion to dwell within the Ultimate Reality of non space and time?"

Souls Leading The Way

"We Are the Lemurian Council of Twelve and we wish to report on the earth changes around you. The earth changes in your world, on your earth, are immense at this time as catastrophic events continue to occur. Gridkeepers, gatekeepers, starseeds and those that know continue to hold the grid in place. The grid continues to radiate the Light of One as each gridkeeper, gatekeeper, lightworker, wayshower, starseed and all others holding that Light of One continue to hold their position within the grid. This grid is filled and ready.

"Let nothing dissuade you from the truth that this New Earth is yours to create new beginnings for all of humanity. We leave you now with this short message knowing that all that hold the Light of One will continue to do so as their soul leads the way."

Souls Playing Games

"The Galactic Federation of Light wishes all to know, the current onslaught of chaos on planet earth will dissipate in time as all older souls holding misthoughts of separation relieve themselves of physical form. This means that as each role is played out to its fullest, each soul holding that form on earth shall complete its stint, so to speak, on earth. After all misthoughts are brought to a head, cleared, cleansed and replaced with higher energetic thought forms, even planet earth shall find itself no longer in physical form but returned to its original star and subsequent vaporous condition.

"It is with the greatest of respect that we as a group of consciousness seeming above the 'level' of human consciousness now relate: all on earth shall continue to undergo massive change until such a point in its evolution is reached to stop the constant cycle of evolution. This means all shall cease to exist on and in planet earth but having further misthoughts of separation continue to play the game of illusion on other planets, etc, in other forms and formless states.

"Yes, we are aware that all is a simultaneous experience but in the experience of many aspects that experience occurs in merely one time/space continuum at a time. Know that as the vibrational state continues to undergo change of greater and greater frequencies, the ability to tap into and experience greater and greater experiences all at one time will increase.

"We leave you now knowing the exact experience your soul chose is the one you now seem to experience, have experienced and shall experience in your so-called time/space illusion."

Spreading The Light Of Truth

"The times before humanity are now filled with more light and love than ever before in its history. We, the Lemurian Council of Twelve, wish all to know it is time for all of humanity to return to its true source of BEing, the Source of One, of all that is and ever will be. This occurrence has not been chosen by as many souls as one would hope, in your realm of illusion, but nevertheless this number of souls now moving forward are more than enough to spread the Light of Truth within the realms of forgetfulness once again.

"All not ready to awaken from the dream of gross distortion shall have yet multiple choices to come to this Light of Truth, in other forms, on other planes of the illusion. And yet, as the illusion comes to a close in this your Golden Age of Oneness and Truth, know that the time to secede is here for those ready to step forward leaving the door open for others to follow at will. This planet and all planets within your illusion are returning to the Light of One regardless of individual souls lost in the maze of forgetting.

"Know that as one who chose to awaken to this truth now it is with the greatest respect that we ask all to be mindful of thoughts, words and deeds to avoid being caught up in the maze of forgetting held by many lost souls."

Stay In Your Own Field Of Consciousness

"Stay in your own field of consciousness. Remember, what you feed your head with during the day moulds your world. Always recall you are a soul that has taken on human form to experience, to express and to expand its own richness; many others in this world are expanding their own richness as well. The ways they perfect this richness may not be the ways you perfect yours. Stay in your own field of consciousness and know each experiences what it has chosen to experience. There is no right or wrong.

"Remember this is an illusion of your own making. Remember the goal is to experience to the utmost level. This may create chaotic times on your earth but be aware, as you are a form of energy you shall attract what your consciousness holds, consciously and unconsciously. Keeping your vehicle clear of unwarranted chaotic action is easier when paying attention to what you allow in your energy field.

"We are the White Winged Consciousness of Nine and we are here to assist those that wish to leave the illusion."

Tapping Into Greater States Of Awareness

"Secure the knowledge of heart's wisdom by listening to those quiet moments of reflection, those moments when the illusory world seems to stop, those times when things go awry, as one would note. For it is during these times that aspects of one's Higher Self shines through the midst of forgetfulness.

"One does not need to question the illusion but to move through it with as much grace and ease as possible, paying no heed to what seems to be happening, unless of course it seems to happen to the subjective mind/body complex in which one experiences earth life. This is not to say, "Stay within yourself and not venture out," but pay attention to what connects with a frequency and when one does not match one's frequency. As these times of cleansing and purging continue, like will continue to attract like energies, frequencies, until all frequencies are balanced within each subjective self and the earth in general. All shall eventually coalesce into One as when the earth experiment began many, many aeons ago in one's time/space continuum.

"Clearly, one does not need to feed discarnate, energetic frequencies but merely pay attention to what is in one's field and clear all misthought, for it is only through clearing misthought that one moves on in awareness to a space in time where there is no misthought, but merely balanced experience and expression adding to soul's journey – whether on earth in form or on other realms in formless states of awareness – until one reaches the final height of Pure BEing once again. Pay no heed to the world in which humanity seems to live unless, of course, it seems to need cleansing and clearing in the subjective life of what seems a single mind/body complex.

"Aspects of Higher Self remain available for all to tap into at will when conditions arise that need clearing, cleansing, transmuting and processing to become free of any misthought. Ask Self and ye shall find the answers to questions ye may have, but know beyond that Self there exists even greater aspects of Consciousness ready to be tapped into at will."

Tapping Into One's Soul Plan

Tapping into one's soul plan becomes easier when in the dream state. To acknowledge soul's needs and desires, pay attention to dreams of a somewhat physical nature. In other words, pay attention to dreams in which you may feel threatened or forced into doing something you do not wish to do; pay attention to dreams where you seem to teach or lecture others and be aware that it is yourself bleeding through to relate a long forgotten soul tool in other lives. This is the way to become fully into soul at all times, by remaining asleep while awake and dreaming the circumstances you wish to participate in while asleep.

This will make more sense to you as you tap further in to soul purpose and meaning.

SAM

The Consciousness Of Oneness Lies Inside

"We are the White Winged Consciousness of Nine here to invite you to stay in your own state of consciousness for all is in Divine Order. Each soul experiences what they have come to experience in physical form. Each soul now moves forward in their physical form's evolution as these cataclysms take place upon your earth.

"Know that the consciousness you seek is already held within you. It is the consciousness of One. This Oneness spreads like wildfire throughout your world, throughout your consciousness. Know that all who seeks to nurture this consciousness are guided and watched over very carefully. We are here to report; you are never alone. You have never been alone. You never will be alone for the Oneness to which many seek lies inside. This Oneness is held by all, yes nourished by few, but held by all upon your earth and beyond.

"As these winter months unfold on your earth, know that each soul now moves forward in its evolution, experiencing either gross disturbances to return to the Oneness or periods of Nirvana and great happiness. For all, the consciousness of Oneness lies inside. This consciousness continues to reveal itself upon your earth. Know for many this may seem difficult to watch as the consciousness, which seems to be outside oneself, unfolds, and evolves through chaos. But recall, each aspect of the whole, which seems in physical form, is merely a part of your own consciousness.

"Once you have secured your own consciousness within your Self, you will know and be aware that when chaos appears before you it is but something that needs to be addressed within your own small self of one. We leave you now with this thought; what needs to be addressed within you will reveal itself in coming months."

Through Chaos Comes Remembering

"We are the White Winged Consciousness of Nine and we are here to report. Your world now moves at a fast and furious pace towards awakening to the truth of Oneness. This Wholeness is forgotten to play ill-gotten games upon earth, the planet many now call home. And yet, these ill-gotten games are ending as they have served their purpose.

"It is time for all to know the Oneness that exists within humanity. Each person met along the path of life is yet part of this Oneness. All are One; all humanity in unique form upon earth are yet also part of the one Creator. This BEingness is now calling forth for humanity to recognize its True Self. Pay attention to, as many would say, the irritations, the reactions, the seeming disruptions within the life one seems to live. Solitary existence is ending once again. Another cycle of humanity's living within unique form is ending. The cycle has come full circle for the last time within this last Golden Age. The return to Oneness will be met through the trials and errors of each unique figment upon your earth.

"The chaos that erupts upon your earth is what you call proof of this return, for through chaos comes remembering. Each calamity, each chaotic event sparks a memory; a compassionate force moves and flows. This remembrance brings all back to the truth that each experience contributes to the return, the awakening of the long forgotten spark within each ones heart's core. The times of forgetting are over for humanity.

"This Golden Age shall end in a glorious display of Oneness. Many upon the earth now will not be within the form they currently experience when this goal comes to fruition. And yet, all now play a role in achieving this glorious event within what you call humanity's game. The time for separation is over. The earth experiment has reaped many rewards and expanded the richness of each unique figment, soul, if you will. But the time for earth's experience for souls is ending with this last Golden Age.

"We greet you now knowing the True Self is and always has been effective and within each one waiting for recognition. Now is the time."

Timeline Jumps

"These wobbles/timeline jumps will assist you in refining your bodies to be more in tune with the bands of consciousness of which many of you now seek. Know that we, the Pleiadians of higher bands of your consciousness, are with you to assist in all aspects as you make these timeline jumps."

Trees of Faith

"Decoration of the New Earth has begun. We are the White Winged Consciousness of Nine here to report. Plant trees of faith in your New Earth, faith in the goodness of humanity as a whole. Plant your trees of faith knowing that all on earth will change quickly now as the turmoil and chaos appears to increase. Know that you and many others hold the keys to this New Earth by cementing these thoughts of faith in humanity within your New Earth. Know that as these days continue to increase to a crescendo of mass confusion those that plant these trees of faith will move further into the Oneness of which humanity truly is. Know that many upon your earth have not chosen to experience this Oneness in this lifetime. Be that as it may, all are part of this Oneness and have never truly left it for in Reality all are part of that thing called *All That Is*. Know that in the dark days ahead the mire of mass confusion will continue for quite some time. But those planting the trees of faith in this New Earth of Oneness will continue to reap the goodness and abundance that humanity now moves toward. Keep the faith in yourselves to do the job you have come to perform and know that all are One everlasting, eternal goodness and Light.

"We are the White Winged Consciousness of Nine and we bid you adieu knowing the faith in your thought form cements the New Earth energies."

Whispers Of Soul Self

"One needs only to open the channels of Love and Light within to hear whispers of Self. Each human holds this Self within the confines of its humanness and it is only through becoming aware of the possibilities that one may access and incorporate whispers from the Soul Self, within each life. All come into life form on earth aware of the possibilities but soon lose conscious awareness as they continue to incorporate non-wisdoms from life experience.

"It is only through tapping into the Soul Self that one may move fluidly through the earth experience knowing all is illusion, an experience to add to Soul's resume, so to speak. As experience after experience continues to reveal to humanity that all is indeed illusion, many shall end the earth game to play on other spheres of consciousness awareness."

Wisdom And Consciousness

"Wisdom and consciousness are rarely exhibited upon earth in the Present Moment, but this is changing rapidly as many on earth relate their experiences of Love and Light, for it is only through relation of these seeming non-physical experiences that one may motor through the matrix of illusion to the Void of Oneness and Truth.

"All aspects of humanity now undergo great change as planetary and cosmic events affect their very fabric of being. All aspects of Oneness now play a role in returning all back to the consciousness of One, without separation. Non-judgment is the key to Oneness as earth days and nights fill with duality. Know that higher realm assistance is always available for those wishing to rise above the turmoil of duality, **for it is only by remaining neutral that one may leave the illusion of time and space to play on other realms of consciousness**. Many souls have allowed themselves to become mired in the duality of power and weakness, of love and hate, of lack and abundance and it is these souls who now awaken to the truth of Oneness, or leave the planet.

"We do not wish to alarm you, but those not adhering to the love of self and all aspects seen, heard, or sensed will become extinct on your earth. It is with the greatest respect that we your Sisters and Brothers of Light ask all to pay attention to dreamless states of consciousness, for that is where one taps into the presence of Source. All other states of dreamtime can be discarded for they merely keep souls in the illusion of separation.

"As all things on earth continue to change at a rapid rate, those holding the aspects of non-judgment, shall carry their vibrations beyond the confines of earth consciousness."

Part Two

~

Author's Experiences

Becoming More In BEingness

I wake again after a night of waking more times than usual the past few days, each time recalling participating in parallel bands of consciousness. And also asking for assistance again from the Pleiadians, Archangel Raphael and all those who assist humans and souls to clear any misthought and perceived blockages from the physical, astral, emotional, ethereal, mental and all other bodies in all time/space associated with this human body's Essence. "Do you wish to channel?" I hear near dawn. This time I silently reply affirmatively.

"You are moving forward, those of you who have agreed to this process of becoming more in states of awareness, in multiple bands of consciousness, in your own BEingness. We come to you now as group consciousness, ready to assist all those now moving through this process, which may be arduous (!!) at best. But know that the end results are glorious and already achieved for those moving through this process, as humans, as souls, as states of BEingness, consciousness, aspects of the totality of *All That Is*.

"These coming days upon your earth will continue to be filled with energies assisting humanity, compliments of what you assume to be your sun."

I get the impression the assisting energies are coming from yet unknown bands of consciousness, perhaps from what many refer to as the Great Central Sun.

"Know that as you move though this process, the knowingness of your awareness changes. This means that those of you who think you know what is occurring may change your mind while moving though this process.

"Bands of consciousness are important. Remember to stay within your own field of consciousness, for moving through this process it is easy to become lost in the maze of which you refer to as the matrix. Ask for guidance from the highest aspect of your Self and know that we, the Group Consciousness of Aspects of *All That Is*, are always with you ready to assist as you wish. As your own consciousness expands within the matrix of your own beliefs, you become more aware of the bands of consciousness that are readily available to tap into at any moment in time. Pay attention to the vibrational range of frequencies within your own energetic field and know that that range changes constantly.

"We are the Group Consciousness Of Aspects Of *All That Is* and we are here to assist as desired."

Changing Human Experience

One of the most wonderful things about being a human is we get to choose our experience through the use of emotion and thought. Each day our experience changes with what we choose to recognize, participate in and subsequently feed. As mass consciousness continues to progress up the spiral of awakening at a rapid and unsteady pace, one is best reminded to return to neutrality, to hold thoughts of what one wishes to see in the world rather than what one does not wish to experience, for what we resist persists. What we choose to focus on becomes our reality and with so many people focusing on one thing that reality manifests much more quickly.

While living in the midst of great change, one may choose to focus on harmony, love, peace and wholeness for all beings, aware of the fact that as souls each has its chosen experiences. And we may or may not be part of that experience. We shall know if we are living with them, they contact us or it seems our experience. We can then choose to move through the experience in our own serene way, or be manipulated by mass media and collective behavior.

We support what we participate in so let us choose to support life-affirming ways to live and experience life. Humans meditating together can help to establish a more peaceful world. Since we are energetically connected to each other at the heart level, we serve the greater whole whether individually or in groups, making efforts much more expansive and powerful. Many groups are committed to planetary harmony and healing in an expanded way, actively upgrading consciousness and facilitating positive outcomes. Find three such groups affecting humanity in positive ways at GlobalCareRooms.org, HeartMath.org and SandraWalter.com/unity.

Other ways to join the shift of human consciousness from instability and discord to balance, cooperation and increased peace thus fear to Love:

Be mindful of collective thought and consciously choose thoughts of Love, Peace, Harmony, Oneness, etc.

Raise your vibrational rate with laughter, singing, meditation, positive thought, etc.

Lead with your heart. Practice ways to feed your heart, such as volunteer work and giving to those in greater need.

Choose Your Reality & Be The Message Within It.

Additional resources are at:

SamIAMproductions.com.

SAM

Chaos' Purpose

"**K**nowing that all things on your earth are illusion, stay in your own field of consciousness to have the best experience. We wish you to know that as things go awry, as you would say, the time has never been better to tap into that Christ Consciousness within each and every individual on earth. The whole purpose of the chaos in your world is to help those not tapped into this Christ Consciousness. For when one questions the happenings one looks beyond their usual way of thinking. One knows this Christ Consciousness lies within as the Divine Spark (vibrant adamantine particle) within each core of each heart begins to waver. Know that as your earth changes, and catastrophes continue at an increased rate, those experiencing catastrophes have agreed as souls to awaken in this manner. Many will continue to leave this earth to awaken in other spaces of time.

"We are the White Winged Consciousness of Nine and we wish you to know assistance is within your own field of consciousness, for no matter what you believe each soul comes into form with its own guidance, with its own guides wholly available and ready to tap into at any moment in the time/space continuum."

Right before waking to ground this message, I was in another dimension of consciousness where humans were looking for places to hide underground to avoid storms. Yesterday it rained all day from dawn until dusk so the painters worked in our halls because they could not begin painting the outside of our building. Thirty-seven years ago, when I first moved here to Fort Lauderdale it only rained for a few minutes or few hours at the most, never all day long. Rains seem more frequent now and the rainy season seems to be months earlier for it used to be in late May or June, and this is February, so the climate is definitely changing.

Energies remain intense, especially for the past two days and I woke yesterday with gross dizziness; thank goodness not quite as bad as when the room was spinning, but bad nevertheless. I did everything I could think of to rid myself of it and returned to sleep after eating some ginger. I then slept most of the day.

Consider The Law Of One During Interactions

Since I have not been channeling as much, now while still between waking and sleep I ask for guidance from my Lemurian family or others within my soul plan. The first message is a personal one but I share it here knowing it resonates with other humans playing this earth game.

"We are the Lemurian Council of Twelve and we are here to guide you through this process. You, as many others, will help from beyond the veil and yet you shall be in physical form. This new form will hold more Light than ever before on your earth, while still maintaining the dense matter of a body. We know it is not your wish to remain on this planet at this time, but we ask you to please consider the sisters and brothers of Light that you are, still in need of the consciousness of One."

The second message begins...

"The return to Oneness is an easy process if one makes it so. And yet, with the egotistical ways of the ego's public persona, it is quite difficult to look upon all others as ones self. This is the process in the Law Of One, as you well know. It is only through seeing another as one's self that this law becomes firmly rooted in your world. Know that as each day passes in your time/space continuum, the Law Of One becomes closer in consciousness for all of humanity, for this Law Of One is a necessary construct to assist with the return to Oneness and end the illusion on earth. We ask that all consider the Law Of One during their interactions with others.

"We are the Lemurian Council of Twelve and we are here to assist and guide those that seek our assistance."

Author's Experiences

Departed Daughter's Message

While working on a new image, the computer begins to do weird stuff until I figure it out. Someone wants my full attention, WOW (my departed daughter's initials – known as Rebecca in the book series) is with me; she knows that tomorrow it will be three years since her physical body's departure and I have been thinking about her a lot.

"Ok, so you have my attention," I say silently. "Go…"

"There is so much love for you Momma. You got to know that. There is so much love. And when in human form we don't always say that. I know I said it to you many times but I want you to feel that love even now, even as you rid yourself of my thought form just as you have done with Daniels (my son who departed before her – his initials were DAD). You have to know you are getting out this time, out of the maze of rebirth, if you like. But again, it is a choice made fully aware when on the other side of life (as a soul) to be out of the game and aware fully of our choices. I want you to know, I am also successfully out of the maze as is DAD and we are both balanced and happy – as much as a soul can be.

I just want you to know, despite your egotic ways trying to drag you down even now, you were the best momma for us both. You are the best person now and we are all – yes, imaginary as you think we are – we are all very proud of you, knowing what you have faced successfully, and I might add, tough it out to stay.

We wish you the best and know it will continue to come for you are worth the best Momma. The New Year will bring you many more changes but this time they will be much more to your liking. Continue to move with the flow. Let everyone learn in their own way and only reach out to them when asked or when you feel compelled to, knowing they need some kind, loving words.

That's it Momma. I leave you with this thought: Don't spend so much time working – again, yes (she is repeating something I have heard before) play, play, play. You know we did!

WOW

Different States Of Consciousness

Each time upon waking I recall being in another dimension. One time, I was in bed at the house on 47th Drive, another speaking into my recorder full of excitement about a book. The cover kept changing as if animated, with faces, first white men with large noses and then black men faces. I was very proud of the title but could not figure out why the recorder was not recording what I was repeating of my 'dream'. At one point, I was agreeing to things while sitting or lying down in another realm, it seemed with beings of higher realms. With each agreement, there was a white line inside some kind of recording device to my right. A paper would appear after the white line and the agreement would then be recorded, one after the other, there were several agreements.

Weird stuff continues to happen as dimensions merge and veils thin. I continue to seek the highest realm possible and highest good of all concerned, even knowing there is no one here but me. I am also continuing to rid the small mind of thought forms by deleting family videos and digital images, quite a task for what used to be a very emotional mother in this life. Two more days until the blood moon and total lunar eclipse with a 12:12 am mid-point and energies are intense as another message flows through the veil of forgetfulness!

"We are the White Winged Consciousness of Nine and we are here to report. As one moves through these times, it is important to remember you are a spirit in human form. It is time to bear witness to the falsities of the 3D world. During these next few months as things ripen to a peak of chaos you shall bear witness to these falsities as the 3D earth finally moves forward in consciousness. This consciousness is more in tune with Gaia as she too steps up, so to speak, matching the vibration more closely in tune with other planets immersed in the Oneness of All.

"These next few months will be cumbersome at best. Those who have prepared, in mind, in physicality, shall move through the process more gracefully. Those not yet awakened will be immersed fully in the chaos and not prepared for what is to come. Remember, this is an experience in the mind of humanity, of which all souls on earth agreed to experience. Moving though these levels, these states of consciousness, one shall find many (people) who are not in tune with their own states of awareness (totally asleep within the dream of this illusion). Allow these precious souls to come to their own conclusions, through their own experiences, and judge them not, for recall each soul has chosen to experience uniquely on this earth. Each experience and each expression of each soul holds a unique signature of a unique soul, having a unique experience in its own small mind, if you will, for lack of a better word.

"During these next few months, before your Summer months arrive, the consciousness on earth shall shift to be more in tune with the Christ Consciousness it is headed for fully. Know, again, not all souls have agreed to awaken to this Christ Consciousness or move into this Christ Consciousness. Albeit, few will move toward this consciousness with the knowledge they are a conscious, sovereign being. As these days and months unfold on your earth, remember, judge not lest ye too fall sway to the separation many souls have chosen to experience.

"We are the White Winged Consciousness of Nine and we wish all to know assistance from your own Higher Self is but a whisper away in your own small mind of one."

Dimensions Of Consciousness

Just had a hell of a night, perhaps due to eating six mini-brownies with some kind of unnatural sweetener. The intestinal distress, mainly gas and much stomach gurgling, was intense and I shall not have as many of the brownies left at one sitting, furthermore, I shall not purchase brownies of this type in the future. It seems that since Amazon bought out the Whole Foods grocery store recipes have changed to cheaper and less organic ingredients.

Up repeatedly to rid the body of gas, at one point, I woke to recall the words "characteristics of thought forms" and decided to tap back into that state of awareness to investigate this term. Yes, we all experience higher realm states of awareness during what is referred to as the 'sleeping state'; and need only to recall certain words to return to them and bring the teaching to our current state of awareness. The following came through upon waking the next time as the body seemed to lift, being lighter and vibrating in a different state than usual (this experience was different from other states of awareness during channeling and I think the month plus break from channeling led me to greater states of awareness).

"Dimensions of consciousness are easily left behind as the human mind forgoes characteristics of each thought form. Each thought form is merely a construct of beliefs taken on when in human form. As this human form changes its beliefs, the constructs that hold these beliefs begin to dissipate (to break apart) into the nothingness from whence they arrived. Ridding ones self of the thought forms upon the earth dimension becomes cumbersome when one is mired in the dramas of everyday life, when one has chosen to experience family life, expressing and experiencing each unique family member in human form. Dimensions of consciousness are easily traveled when the thought forms of earth are left behind.

"Each thought form holds unique aspects. Upon dissipation, each thought form shatters (breaks apart) as unique aspects are separated from it. Take, for instance, the thought form of your body. The body holds many constructs, the arms, the legs, brain, organs, heart and so forth. Taking each of these and doing away with them in the mind, allowing the body to become an ethereal form without organs, without arms or legs, without feet or eyes or hands, etc., helps to rid one of this construct that can be limiting when traveling in other dimensions of awareness.

"Each dimension holds clues to the humans awakening. Traveling these dimensions is easily done in the sleeping state as one dissipates the human thought form to move through dimensions as not a human but as an experience, as an experience had in mind, the small mind of one. This can be the beginning step to moving into greater states of awareness, for it is only when one leaves behind the human form that greater states of awareness are achieved.

"We leave you now with this thought: the characteristics of each thought form must be thoroughly dissipated to move through increasing states of awareness beyond your earth."

There is no name for this source but I get the impression the message comes from a mass of consciousness that has not experienced life in human form nor as souls.

Upon reading though this channel I get that we come in to experience and express unity consciousness through separation and when that experience and expression has reached its fullness, we once again return to the true Unity of Oneness, never to experience life on earth in separate form again.

Now, after a two-plus hour nap after eating breakfast, having waked only 90 minutes earlier, there is a slight headache. We are headed toward another lunar or solar eclipse along with a full blood moon, as they call it, and energies continue to be very intense. What a joy to have the freedom to do as I please and care for myself rather than push this body to work and make money for an exaggerated rent fee. Yes, finally the Universe is taking care of all financial needs without physical effort on my part!

Author's Experiences

Ego Acting Out Separation As Family Chaos

The following all came upon waking at four o'clock in the morning, amid increased gastric activity *(everything in parentheses with italics are my thoughtful additions)*.

From what may be considered a higher perspective, all thoughts are the illusion of the believer. So why does one imagine chaos in family members? These aspects of self must be embraced wholly to dissipate all thoughts of separation *(egos belief, continuing to believe in separation it believes these aspects must now be incorporated, thereby keeping one in the matrix of illusion.)*.

"Based on one aspect of consciousness, one may say these chaotic events occur to assist those involved with balancing all experiences within the field of consciousness, while seeming to be a unique aspect lost in the matrix of illusion *(meaning balancing karmic-filled lives as an soul, but on the other hand, allowing ego to keep one locked in the maze by believing in separation)*. These aspects are now returning to full consciousness, life by life, in a much condensed manner as the ethers thin, for experience is now condensing into what appears to be denser and more tightly packed slots of time.

"As time continues to advance into the dissipation of nothingness, meaning as time continues to dissipate by condensing experience in more densely packed moments, the chaotic events occur more rapidly, with results happening much sooner in the spectrum of time than in previous years, aeons, if you will. And as each moment of chaos continues to seem to affect what appears as 'others' outside oneself, the incorporation of these 'others' continues at a rapid pace when one acknowledges the aspects within *(meaning aspects of ego, creating separation through what appears as people)* that make these illusions possible.

"Allow what seems outside your self to unfold in its own manner. Stay clear of the chaos as much as possible and know each event occurs and unfolds as directed by higher aspects of consciousness. We know this seems confusing but seeming to be a separate aspect, apart from 'others' makes this possible. For as you stand back and watch things unfold, you also give up the notion of control or involvement.

"Remember, all aspects of the Whole continue to exist with egos in place that strive to keep souls in a state of separation. Accepting that what seems as 'others' is really an aspect of other parts of your own ego will help you through what appears as family members acting out against the very loved ones that have nurtured them for years, throughout life, and now seem to be acting out against the love of *(their own)* self.

"Remember, the illusion of your matrix continues to build and dissipate with emotion and thought. Continue the practice of loving what appears as a unique self, and allow the rest to disappear. *(Radiate love throughout what seems to be the physical body and out into the field of consciousness, without focusing on individual aspects of consciousness. For when one focuses on individual aspects, one cements them in consciousness and feeds the thought of separation.)* We know this is not easy to do nor understand but, as you note to others, remain in the flow. Do not seek outside the flow that continues to surround what appears as your own state of consciousness.

"We are aspects of your (Higher) Self assisting as required by your own egotic consciousness."

It seems that following beliefs/information in *A Course in Miracles* will be best to do as egotic aspects of consciousness play their hand in the card game of life.

Forming Group Consciousnesses

While compiling information for a class, it occurs to me that as one's consciousness increases while in physicality, the ability to tap into even greater states of awareness increases as well.

If we define states of awareness to include a soul and Higher Self (monad), then we can tap into bands of consciousness higher than the soul. First, we connect with our soul to incorporate all experiences and expressions. We are then able to unify with other souls to form group consciousnesses of which can be in and out of physical form.

While still in human form the Law of Attraction determines what group of consciousness we resonate with to power further thought forms. This is what is happening on a grand scale now as more people unify with Oneness consciousness, while others continue to play the game of duality and separation.

Examples of conglomerations of different souls forming a group consciousness while out of physicality would be The White Winged Consciousness of Nine or The Lemurian Council of Twelve. These group consciousnesses contain souls that have lived upon the surface of earth within this illusion; however, they are still thought forms.

Having tapped into Higher Self and merged all those lower aspects of consciousness, one then has the ability to move on to even greater states of awareness, merging with other Higher Selves, Monads if you will, to form a group consciousness consisting of a conglomeration of Higher Selves. There is no end to this illusion; it is just that one continually reaches greater and greater states of awareness within all that is, was and ever shall be. And so the game continues in other states of awareness.

Can we tap into a band of consciousness that is not a thought form?

As long as we are thinking with a human mind, the answer is no. We are always tapping into thought forms, thought forms using what is known from the experience and expression of a soul or Higher Self, even if of group consciousness. Thought is not the final *Pure BEing*, which bears no description nor seeks. Yet, some people can fleetingly tap into the state of *Primordial Awareness* during deep meditation. Consciousness changes even though *Primordial Awareness* is (as noted by Sri Nisargadatta Maharaj in his book *I AM THAT*) in every state; *Primordial Awareness* is without parts, beginningless and endless.

SAM

From There To Here

Journaling became unnecessary after beginning to channel and mold old notes into published books. But at the start of 2012, everything changed very quickly. My physical host cried out asking, "What the hell happened? If everything is an illusion as I've come to believe, and I mold this world with thought, why am I now home-base less? Or shall I refer to it as home free?"

Yeah, home is where I am. I am my own home. And yet, the world suddenly seemed so uninviting, strange and threatening. "How can my own consciousness be drawing this energy?" I asked repeatedly. How did my consciousness move from a completely remodeled, suburban, waterfront home, surpassing all visioning, to an urban seedy extended stay hotel? Deep inside I knew it served a greater purpose.

I'd never choose (as a human) to live as I have or continue to do. On a physical level, thoughts carried me out of limitation to freedom, out of lack to abundance, out of dis-ease to physical and mental wholeness. However, my personality's soul chose various experiences as part of the program to complete the cycle of time on earth, and perhaps other dimensions of space and time as well. So, how did I get from 'there' to 'here'? It all seemed to begin in 2011...

Author's Experiences

Many people follow the path to Oneness (which we left only in the small mind of one). Nudges indicating an upcoming move increased drastically throughout the summer of 2011. Dreams foretold flooded areas. A freak tornado tore through the neighborhood as I watched in awe of Mother Nature's beauty. Rats began to eat birdseed from my treasured bird feeder. Empty for nearly three years, the house next door filled with noisy neighbors.

Cries from the large, tropical potted tree in the living room (to join Mother Nature and prosper) move me to action and I soon watch as my now 19-year-old grandson Samuel lovingly plants it in the front yard. Friends and family benefit when I give away Florida mango, Brazilian papaya and Mexican Noni trees, grown from organic seeds, now too big for their pots after sensing a future move. It saddens me to know I shall never partake of their wholesome bounty.

Many lightworkers dispose of history in earnest during the winter months. Beliefs change yet again along with a great urge to forego old customs and ways of living. We end holiday traditions to begin ones of our own or, as in my case, to enjoy the time alone out of 3D drama.

The New Year brings an entire month of vastly, disrupted Internet and telephone service. Working becomes less important because there's no way to put messages online without leaving my beautiful, safe sanctuary. An increasing urge to clean house spurs me into much more physical action. Getting rid of as many belongings as possible is no longer difficult for the past four years served to help me break free of many beliefs no longer serving a new state of BEing. Many previously valued possessions soon sit in new homes with family, friends or charities.

Over the course of the next few months, many pots of organic vegetables fill with tiny, black flies. A pattern of planting vegetable seeds, nurturing them, and subsequently dumping them before harvest again prompts thoughts of moving. "Yes," I think fighting the thought as quickly as it comes, "it's almost time to leave this beautiful sanctuary for the area is too metropolitan."

Dreams of floods continue even after news reports note flooded areas. Sounds of emergency vehicles increase dramatically, often waking me from sound sleep. City workers install a new monitoring camera blocks away as I watch from under the huge, shady, organic mango tree next to the canal on which my rented sanctuary sits. And then city officials' telephone to test a new emergency broadcast system and I wonder how they got my number for few people have it.

DAD's transition fueled the fire for the end of life, as I knew it. Recognizing the signs of change is now much easier than before. I adapt more easily than in younger years but am still not fond of change because everything in my life changed drastically over the last six years. Throughout this nagging feeling of upcoming change in late 2011, I remain ever grateful for my beautiful home, offering thanks many times a day. This too nags at me for I recall reading somewhere that when things are really good we're ready to move on to greater opportunities.

This prompts me to recall a book read several years ago. We must divorce ourselves from the concerns of living in the everyday world, Dennis William Hauck notes in *The Emerald Tablet: Alchemy for Personal Transformation* (AlchemyLab.com), to cleanse completely all traces of psychic impurities like ego, dissolving the current personality to morph into yet another new form, aligned with Divine Will, the higher truth. Yes, as many others note, we must die to be reborn closer to our original form of Light.

Hauck notes eight steps to freedom. Soul realizes the illusions it embraced and we begin to rid ourselves of clutter during Calcination, Step One. This is the beginning of a black stage in our life where denser energies (attachments, possessions, ego, interest in the material world) burn away to reveal our true essence.

Further breaking down of the artificial structures of the psyche occurs in Dissolution, the second step. Releasing pent-up emotional energies, recognizing and showing our wounds, instead of burying emotions, which masks or warps our true nature, occurs. This process affords us the opportunity to become more feeling instead of closed, to let go of control and break habits. It results in a flowing presence free of inhibition, projection, prejudgment, and restrictive mental structures.

Step Three is Separation from the ego where the merging of soul and spirit offers a newly acquired vantage point to drive our spiritual transformation. During this more conscious process, we review formerly unconscious material and decide what to reintegrate into our persona. Our true essence begins to shine through as we use intuition more, continuing to release anything that does not serve the greater good or us. We abandon destructive habits and behavior patterns and let go of what is no longer relevant or useful.

A "harmonious marriage of soul and spirit" occurs in the fourth step of Conjunction. This is where we set things right and empower our true selves. We unite the masculine and feminine sides of our personalities increasing intuitive insight. Synchronicities confirm that we are on the right track as we create a unified self true to inner essences and universal truths.

Mental images or visions now seem more representative of reality than anything our eyes see during Step Five, Fermentation. Hauck notes we yearn to tell others of our discovery and spread our vision of higher consciousness. Divine passion and inspiration springs forth to raise us to a new level of being. Periods of fasting, deeper meditation and intense prayer, activated imagination, or other activities that further breakdown the personality occur. Some people refer to this step as the dark night of the soul.

Step Six, Distillation, demands the utmost purification as we cut ourselves off from our identity. It consists of reflective techniques to raise ones psyche to the highest level possible, free from sentimentality and emotions. Distillation marks "death of the old ego and the rebirth of the transpersonal Self."

During the next step (Coagulation), heightened energy, peace of mind and the ability to survive any onslaught with greater adaptability to new situations ensues. A permanent state of consciousness embodies the highest aspirations and evolution of mind allowing us to use this presence to transform the reality of everything around us. This realization of the eternal spirit body, often confirmed in what many refer to as out-of-body experience, is "achieved first only in hypnagogic and semi dream states" but becomes solidified light that seems more real than physical bodies. Feelings and intuition surface to help us stay connected to the newly discovered Presence within.

The Eighth Step takes us back to where we started therefore "setting things right." We "return empowered and embodied in an incorruptible higher consciousness."

My small mind of one tells me even though I thought this process completed, it's time to do it all over again. For each time we go though the process we find greater insights into the Self of I AM.

Reassessment mode includes shedding old and lower vibrating relationships, material possessions, and out of date self-perceptions. In the wee hours of early January 2012, I often find myself waking, to hear guidance leading me out of bed to dispose of memorabilia, things that prompt memories of a life left behind. Although consciously forgotten, their energy remains in my pristine and safe sanctuary. Clearly, I think, it's time to rid myself, completely and consciously, of all ties to the past. Spring-cleaning helps to accomplish this task.

In late January 2012, I shred journal entries and memories used to write the first three books. Stacks of medical records and x-rays, evidence of three incurable conditions and a long list of issues formerly treated with thirteen prescriptions, soon sit shredded in the garbage days later. Debit and charge cards, airline and other membership cards, all end up in the trash after cutting them with scissors. I save one credit card knowing it is a necessary evil to wade through the illusion.

The previously treasured 40+ year-old *Bible* and others books, along with lots of other material possessions unnecessary for the new world consciousness of Oneness sit safely in the trash bin, to be discarded for good on trash day. Finally, after eons of forgetfulness, I've risen from the human mind delusion of birth and death certificates, marriage, divorce, medical history, and other limiting beliefs that locked me in horrendous conclusions.

One photo album (out of ten left behind in 2007 – delivered by family members along with other things to my new sanctuary) sits shredded in the garbage in early February 2012. And then I shred my departed son's (known as Daniel in previous books) birth and death certificate in one fell swoop before destroying his baby teeth, lock of hair and baby books.

Many days find me sorting through, and boxing more clothes, books, and other things to give away to family, friends, and charities. Thoughts of ending this illusion of duality soon become urgent. At one point, it's clear that I'm not doing family or the world any favors by gifting them with things. We do not need to remember and continue to feed energies that serve separation. An entire set of pristine encyclopedias from the early 1970's soon sits ripped up in the trash bin. Now I realize how lucky people are to lose all possessions suddenly, through acts of nature or other means. At least they don't have to consciously let them go.

Intuition now guides me to override my preference not to order things online. Since online orders require use of a credit card, I stopped shopping that way upon living in my new sanctuary. But the only way to solve an issue with the most used computer, my 2006

Gateway laptop (used only for work and never online activity), requires a new battery and adaptor that is only available online. I also take the Gateway to my treasured $30 an hour local computer guru to fix an issue with memory.

And then something guides me to dust the unused second bedroom. Even though my time is best spent doing things other than cleaning, the reason quickly becomes clear. It's the major push to further freedom. Black mold sits at the bottom edge of a large clothes dresser. Upon emptying and dragging the heavy wood cabinet outside, I see black mold covering the entire dresser bottom. It seeped up from the beautiful tile floor, penetrated the blue carpet, and spread from the middle of the dresser to cover the carpet beneath it as well.

Since the house owner lives in the Philippines, I telephone his friend who fortunately lives blocks away. The rest is history – which I really do not care to claim for it's not really a part of the true 'me' – but I'm documenting this for those with feet firmly planted upon the path back to the Oneness that we never really left to begin with.

By the time the first dreaded email comes, I've already disposed of half a room of clutter. The house owner thanks me for making it possible for his family to build two homes in the Philippines and sell one but now it's time for me to move. He's decided to sell the house. Of course, as many times before, he announces, I can buy it and not have to move in a month. He

Author's Experiences

soon agrees to abide by our agreement to give one another two-month's notice.

Upon renting the house that he tried to sell for $360K in 2008 (when I leased it), and over the course of my stay, I knew home ownership was not for me. Now the house's value is less than $80K but the owner adamantly prices it to sell at $118K. Later, I learn he knew there was a mold issue when he purchased the house in 2004.

Most of the mold disappears after two weeks of dousing it with a bleach solution, scrubbing and drying the carpet with fans. It never occurs to me that guidance to change the lease from yearly to monthly makes a difference. Surely, the recent decision to stop paying rent several months in advance will not affect this outcome. Surely, I will be able to stay here after convincing the owner that it's the best thing for both of us. Alas, the owner is not convinced and in a whirlwind 36-hours, after phoning my daughter – her initials were WOW – in a panic, my family, firmly rooted in 3D reality, helps me pack up and move.

Thus begins, once again, the process of dissolving the current personality to morph into yet another new form, aligned with Divine Will.

SAM

Fruits Ripen From Past Labors

"**W**e are the Lemurian Council of Twelve and we are here to report. Do you wish to channel?"

I reply affirmatively and ask them to stay, while still on the cusp of sleep and reaching for the tape recorder.

"Sisters and brothers of Light you are moving through your realms of consciousness quickly. The days before you now lead into your 2020, the time where fruits will ripen from past labors. This is a time of great joy for us beyond those realms of which you call yours, for all advance together. Know that as you move through these stages of the Great Awakening as the co-creators that you are; we are with you all the way. The Sisters and Brothers of Light are cheering you on knowing the Great Awakening is taking place for those that wish it to be so.

"We the Lemurian Council of Twelve caution you to invite only the aspects of Oneness, to avoid those aspects of separation in your mind, for it is only in the small mind of one that the aspects of separation exist. Know that as you move through this process of the Great Awakening, the separation you appear to be faced with are only aspects of the small self wishing to be acknowledged, nurtured and welcomed. For there is no darkness, there is no light. There is only Oneness, the one True BEingness within the illusion that seems apart from the Void.

"We leave you now with this thought: As the light and darkness merge more fully, as the small minds gather into One, will you serve your role as chosen by your soul before birth or will you step back into the realms of separation to yet another circle on your wheel of life?"

Goddess Of Wisdom

Sometimes when unexpected electrical mishaps occur, such as movies ending abruptly, forwarding to the end as if an unseen hand clicks on the computer's mouse to end the movie, I intuitively sense a channel coming through and take out the laptop to ground it...

"There is not much time left for you to do what you came to do, to accomplish what you failed as a human to accomplish aeons ago. The time is ripe and you are ready to deliver these most important messages of your soul's plan. I am the Goddess Of Wisdom and I am ready to again speak through you if you are willing to bump up your channeling skills a notch. This is a planned event from higher realm energies already known to you. You are the Goddess Of Wisdom in yet another form and I ask you to be aware of this as you move about your day for soon, very soon, your world will again be turned upside down. This state of affairs will not affect you physically but it will affect you mentally and emotionally, if you allow it to. Remember, you are a soul who came to earth in mind, yet again, to experience life in physical form. But this is not who you are. You are not even the past incarnation of the Goddess Of Wisdom but I ask you to allow this energy to channel through you and to help your now physical form to assist humanity and you alone as you move though the maze of forgetting.

"It seems our energies are quite a bit off at this point but the more you allow me to come through you the more we shall be in synch with one another."

Text continues to jump above and merge with previous lines as I type into the computer making it difficult to concentrate for fear of not being able to piece it all together and therefore losing the channel.

"I am the Goddess Of Wisdom, one of your very own incarnations in mind, thought form, and I am now here to help as assigned by your own soul."

Now I get the idea that there will be family turmoil.

PS: Two years later, after sitting back to watch family turmoil unfold and clear, the decision to channel primarily groups of consciousness, higher realms on the scale of evolution than single soul expressions or Ascended Masters, cements while facilitating classes at a local Theosophical Society. Much turmoil seems apparent in the world... this too shall pass but the most notable constant seems to be exhaustion. Yet, there always seems enough time to do what must be done and for the most part move with ease and grace while allowing certain body parts to release what they need to release without interference.

Gold Comes After Listening

"The Oneness that your soul seeks is already yours. You have only to recognize this in all aspects...you have only to play this out in your own illusion..."

Again, I am guided to set aside time every day to listen, but still do not. I have so many books in draft, I tell myself, and they are really just for me and there is nothing new to say. But people are beginning to become quite interested in my Internet posts and out of perhaps 1,000 people who like and or share the work, one will buy a book or two... I waffle between balancing all aspects to thinking this is just a hologram of illusion that can be dissipated when everyone, all my aspects, recognize it for what it is, as in *The Matrix* movie.

The following message came before I finally rolled out of bed to start the day.

"Imagine being so powerful that there are so many aspects of yourself that you can't count them all. This is you! Imagine, if you will, an energy so powerful that it literally has aspects of itself in and out of the illusion, playing various games, and yet one aspect of that Self remains to call all others home when the experiment, the expression, the experience has reached its accumulation point, having experienced and expressed all aspects of itself. This is what is occurring now with humanity as all return back to that original Source BEing of One; first individually and then coalescing and merging once again into that one Void, that one unit, that one No-Thing, the Oneness of all."

So now, as I transcribe the tape an hour later, I set time aside to also listen for a message and, of course, it comes...

"One has only to set time aside, as you know, to hear the wisdom of ones very own soul. For it is, after all, only your illusionary soul that seeks expression on what you refer to as earth. Be that as it may, we, being other aspects of your Self, do seek to coalesce and end the game of life on earth for the final time. We are cheering you on, that aspect that seems so alive on earth; the one chose above all other aspects of its own self to represent the one balancing all aspects, to assist in the imaginary return to something never left. Yes, it is only while seeming to be in the game of earth life that one needs to find ways to end the illusion.

"But we advise you to be careful about beliefs that all is illusion and one need do nothing. For in the illusion it is necessary to balance aspects and end the game. So again, we, aspects of yourself, ask you to address those that seek you out, those that are in your face, so to speak, asking for direction or guidance. And we ask that you merely step aside of your ego to assist them in their own balancing. That is all we have to share at this time.

"Thank you for taking the time to listen."

Heart Opening

"You are moving to a time beyond your current dimension. We, the White Winged Consciousness of Nine, are here to assist you on your journey. We know this process is not easy for the human form in which you inhabit at this time. We know too that you do not wish to be in this form, but we ask that you continue as you have, to know unseen realms of which you too are part of in another space and in other times guide you.

"We ask you to remember, it is a human experience but it is also an experience of soul growth, of coming to know not only that of which you are not but returning to the Source Of All Things, knowing that it is One BEing Of Light, Of Darkness, Of All Things. We shall assist you on other levels at other times. Pay attention to the clues that continue to come into your life and know you are never alone."

Now facing what seems the reality of body hardware issues, heart singing (gross heart opening) – the most beautiful song ever heard – as I wake before dawn feeling as if the heart itself has a rather large hole in it, which it now breathes through! I shall rest as required, do what I can and just generally make it as easy on myself as possible. As a human diagnosed with several heart conditions in the past, it could be a scary process but I remain steadfast in my belief that this, as many other so-called symptoms, will pass. We shall see as I ask the

Pleiadians, my Higher Self and all those who resonate with Light and Love to assist in the process of clearing, cleansing and transmuting all misthought from all bodies in all so-called realities of the time/space continuum.

Moving Into Christ Consciousness

"Those that wish to do so now move into a higher level of consciousness on your earth. Many are experiencing a fluey feeling that is not the usual flu or cold. These are signs of raising the body's frequency with light codes now coming into earth. Know that as each human body assimilates these light codes the body must make its own adjustments. Some may feel as if they have the flu, a cold or combination of both. Some may experience periods of great body heat with a subsequent cooling down period. Still others may seem to experience headaches, body aches, or changes in eating and sleeping habits. These are common occurrences when human bodies assimilate light codes subsequently changing the DNA within physical frames. Know that as your earth continues to change its frequency those upon her choosing to move into this Christ Consciousness, this light-filled DNA consciousness, shall continue to experience these changes within the physical frame.

"Not all have chosen to move into this consciousness of One. It is of the utmost importance to be patient with those that have not chosen, in this lifetime, to move into Christ Consciousness. All souls choose before birth; these choices are not made after birth. All souls come in to experience and express uniquely in each life. Those willing to undergo this process of souls do so through a group consciousness, as souls determining, striving to experience and express the Christ Consciousness together.

"We are the White Winged Consciousness of Nine and we wish you to know, not all experience is chosen as a soul, for the free will of humans can lead to unique experiences not planned for. Know that as humanity continues to raise its frequency chaos erupts, for through chaos Nirvana is reached. Know that each soul moves through this experience and expression as a human with the knowledge that there will be subsequent lives, if not in human form in other expressions of experience and frequencies. Be grateful for this gift of human life and now the changes as your winter months unfold. Know that each unique human you see has chosen to experience and express life on your earth at this time of the Grand Awakening and the return to Christ Consciousness for all."

There is a little bit of heart pain now, after waking repeatedly with excess body heat and subsequent cold.

Multi-Generational Beliefs

After asking for a message upon waking, I heard the words "Multi-Generational." The message begins as I listen.

"We are those aspects of you yet unrecognized . Humanity now moves quickly through multi-generational beliefs. These beliefs have held  humanity back for a very, long, time. These beliefs are now being brought forth into the mainstream of humanity's thought. As these beliefs continue to raise, the chaos on your earth increases. And yet, all is, as you say, in Divine Order as this Divine Timing allows more aspects of humanity to process and clear misthoughts from multi-generations.

"As humanity moves through this process of clearing these misthoughts, these patterns of thoughts that are in error, as many would say, know that each mirror presented carries a belief to be considered. Know that as one considers this belief, the belief of multi-generations, it is time to clear misthoughts within the matrix of illusion.

"Remember, humanity is but an aspect of *All That Is*, the void of darkness, in dense physical form now returning to lighter aspects of its own self to clear, process, cleanse, transmute all misthought and return to the Wholeness that it is. This is in humanity's game a long process. Once Wholeness is achieved in all aspects the game continues, changing, moving toward that aspect of consciousness that never left the Mother Void."

Humanity now begins to uncover darker aspects of duality, gross misuse and abuse of children as many watch the process of discovery in sheer disgust, creating more compassionate humans as disclosure continues to unfold on a massive scale.

Phases Of Chaos

Mass hysteria has now taken over much of the planet with food and sundries shortages, due to hoarding (imagine no toilet paper!), government mandated shutdowns and other disruptions, all due to a newly named virus. Of course, those tapped into higher frequencies experience it as a way to help humanity awaken. And on yet another dimension/experience, this is an elite planned event to change the financial system globally, for it collapsed in 2008 but that fact has been covered up for fourteen years. On the cusp of sleep after taking a short nap, I sense a message along with the now familiar increase in body frequency so I turn on the laptop near my side to record it.

"Your world spins out of control as this first phase, planned by your leaders, occurs. It is in the best interest of all those on earth to adhere to the guidelines voiced by these 'officials' as you move through this process for it includes many stages and steps. By this we the Galactic Federation of Light mean, pay attention to the voiced instructions givens by 'leaders' and find your place of comfort and security, while humanity moves through the awakening process, through chaos and confusion.

"Remember, staying safe in your home is a means to avoid undue hardship when things become chaotic to the point where mass consciousness no longer obeys the 'rule' of leaders."

I get the impression they are speaking of this Summer, noting it will be even more crucial to remain at home (something I have not been doing while attending and facilitating classes at the local Theosophical Society) and out of the possibility of chaos. This may mean, further lifestyle changes, riots, etc., and a mandatory yet temporary disruption in classes.

"Now on to phase two of the process, this includes everlasting effects on those wishing to avoid the planned eruption (of the newly named virus). This phase will permanently alter those accepting the 'cure' to the extent that they shall not think consciously."

I ask for clarification.

"By this we mean, those accepting the 'cure' shall be permanently brain altered due to substances within the formula given through intravenous administration. Try as one might, they will be unable to think as clearly as before the 'cure'.

"Phase three includes further restrictions to your society as a whole and it is during this phase that we shall begin to make our presence known."

Personally, I have never believed 'aliens' will make their presence known and this thought pops into my brain as I continue to keep the higher frequency connection.

"Yes, we know, as a single human, you do not believe this will occur, but we ask you to consider your own roots (Lyrian), your own experienced realities (currently known as Talia from the planet Nibiru) and recall the veils of illusion are lifting. As these veils lift, multidimensional experiences increase, as you are well aware, and within these dimensions we the Galactic Federation of Light exist."

Now I understand as I continue to experience living other realities of this life and other lives, mainly in dreams.

"Putting disbelief aside, turn to your fellow humans to find solace from the chaos that erupts during this phase three. For many will not be ready to accept multidimensional existence. This will occur in the what you would refer to as the 'tail end' of your own human experience. For as a soul, we are aware of your choice to leave sooner rather that later, upon completing your mission to balance your own human experience, leave the so-called earth experience and move on in the illusion to other experiences of service to humanity and higher realms of existence."

"We are not here to affect your or anyone's soul plans, but we are here to insure that humanity has a choice on what occurs within their own soul. As soul plans change, upon each human's free will, we are here to insure that each human knows there is a choice."

Physicality's Game Changes, Yet Again

Why do we persist in remaining in physical form when we (as spirit) have no need to?

This question arises as we move closer to 2020 where many more people shall leave the planet, no longer a match for its constantly changing frequency.

One might ask the question above if one continues to remain in physicality.

What then is the role of such a person?

Is it to cement further the rising state of Oneness and Christ Consciousness?

Is it to cause pause for thought through aberrant energy pointing out what needs to change?

Or is it, by choice made before taking on physical form, to assist those who seem lost in the maze of increasing deceit and denial of Oneness?

One must choose to remain within the force of Oneness by actions, by thoughts, emotions and words matching that state of which they wish to experience. For it is only experience and expression of the soul for all to partake of here on earth. Allow higher realm energies, so to speak, your own Higher Self to lead the way as these days and nights morph into unrecognizable states.

SAM

Stay Clear In Your Intention

"Stay clear in your intention in the endeavors you wish to take. We, the White Winged Consciousness of Nine, are with you to assist as these intentions mold your New World. Each endeavor holds the vibration of an intention and it is that intention that creates the reality in which you live. If you intend to fill your New Earth with greater states of awareness, you must change your thought forms to reflect this state of living. This is a step towards the BEingness all ethereal forms lived in for aeons of time on the earth of old before it became filled with the gross distortion of thought forms it now rids itself of today.

"We now take our leave knowing the thought forms you choose to employ will be the very ones that assist the New Earth."

It has been a very, very rough night of repeatedly waking every two hours with intestinal distress to urinate, drink cold water, wipe watery eyes, a runny nose and replace a cold bottle of water under and between breasts to cool down that area, which continues to overheat at night. (Yes, there is another wide gap in the sun creating a steady stream of energy from it to earth and surrounding planets.) Also, I vividly recall being on other dimensions of reality, specifically with James and the young boy we seem to have birthed. I recall a standing James taking a drag from a marijuana cigarette as the shirtless young boy and I lay on the floor next to him. And I recall

Author's Experiences

voicing how his action was inappropriate in front of the child.

Sometimes in the morning during and after these rough nights, I sense downloads, an energy field envelopes my body and I sense downloads coming into me, so I lay there until the energy and downloads dissipate.

Storm Originations, Destinations, Love And Light

As rain continues to fall at a rapid rate, more frequently after the usual rainy season than ever before, I ask for clarification on the cusp of waking.

"Pay attention to where storms originate. Pay attention to where storms flow. Storms are thought forms, consciousness/energy of the people within areas that they originate from and that they flow to. This consciousness fills with the energy/thoughts that are dense and need to be cleared from humanity. This denseness, these thought forms, flow to areas filled with dense thoughts, areas that need to be cleansed of dense energy, for it is only when an area is empty and there's a void that the  consciousness of Truth, of Love and Light can flow in to fill that void. When areas fill with the denseness of consciousness, duality, and separation there is no room for the Oneness of Love and Light to flow.

"It is only through clearing and cleansing of denseness that the void becomes possible to be filled with Oneness and Light. So as humanity continues to clear, to cleanse denseness of duality, storms shall continue, heighten, and shall increase until all denseness is cleared and the void is filled with the Love and Light of Oneness, of Truth, of the Consciousness, the Reality from whence humanity first arrived. For it is only when the Oneness of Love and Light is achieved for all of humankind that the illusion will end. And although one seems in individual form, it is all one Consciousness, many contributions to one Consciousness within the maya of the illusion of the mind/body/spirit system.

Thought Forms Guide Human Experience

"And so it is my friends we find you in the midst of darkness. The treasures you seek are within the world in which you inhabit. As you move through this process of awakening to the Oneness of which you truly are, look upon each aspect of the Whole as yourself. Know that as you move through this process, we the Lemurian Council of Twelve are with you always to guide, to assist, to answer any questions you may have. We are you in another form, in another frequency of time and space.

"Knowing the ultimate reality that all time and space is illusion you may move through this process more fluidly if you understand the issues, the experiences, the consequences you face as a result of your choices of free will are yours alone. The cause and effect in your world is experienced by each individual based upon their free will, using the thought forms they employ within their own mind. We are here to announce to all, the thought forms in which you believe are the thought forms that guide your experience. And we wish you to know your experience changes when the thought forms within your mind change.

"These thought forms are affected not only through the experience you currently move through but through the experiences of your total Essence in other frequencies of being. You may tap into these other frequencies, higher, lower, if you will, for lack of a better word, by meditating in a calm manner and asking to tap into those thought forms of which it is time to alleviate, to let go, to dissipate back into the Void of all possibilities. Know that as you move through this process in these coming days, in these coming months, in these coming years, assistance to reach into your very own Essence to dissipate the thought forms now outdated and no longer needed are all within you.

"We ask all to be patient with each thought form as it appears seemingly in your own private world. For each thought form is now ready to be dissipated, to be removed from the causes and effects that create the experiences in 3D and 4D realms of existence. Know that all move through this process in their own time. Many shall not choose to dissipate, to alleviate, to remove outdated concepts, outdated thought forms, for many people on your earth are not ready to awaken to their own magnificence as creators, as co-creators in a wonderful paradise of Oneness.

"Those that are ready to move into this Oneness more fully may choose to alleviate, to dissolve those thought forms keeping humanity in separation. Any thought form not based in Love is now no longer constructive in the reality of those moving fluidly toward the Oneness of all BEingness. Know that as you move though this process, those needed to assist you in alleviating these constructs of thought forms will appear in your field of consciousness. As each appears, accepting it fully with Love, as part of one's self, assists in the process of recognizing all is but illusion in the singular mind of each seeming human form. Alleviating the constructs of thought forms is easily done upon accepting each form seeming outside oneself as a part of the self, waiting to be recognized and accepted as part of the wholeness of the self and *All That Is*. Know that moving through this process is a Garden of Eden for those enlightened to the ways of Oneness.

"We leave you now with this thought:

"Are you, as your own thought form, ready to remove the constructs of all the thought forms that hold you within the illusion of separation?

"We are the Lemurian Council of Twelve and we are with you always for we are you in yet another frequency of time and space having removed many thought forms and yet we too are a thought form in a reality of the illusion."

Rough night last night and it seems my hours have changed as I continue to prepare for the annual Spring family trip. Hours are still wildly erratic as naps and eating habits continue to change but I do seem to be rising a bit earlier.

So what I understand from this channel just received is that each person we meet, we know, is a part of the Whole, a part of ourselves, a part of the Oneness just at a different frequency. Each individual has its own frequency and experience. Accepting this knowing each human is a part of ourselves, a part of the Wholeness of which we all are, we can allow everyone to have the experience we came in as humans to have, without interfering with that experience, unless we feel called to do so being in the frequency of that particular thought form.

Each frequency that we relate to is the one that we are drawn to balance within our own mind, within our own experience. And so the Law of Attraction continues to work even as we unknowingly move through the process of gathering parts of our self to balance all experience in the illusion of this earth. For as we move though this final Golden Age, each unique thought form and frequency shall balance in one point of time and space to return to that frequency of Oneness, of LOVE. I am not sure if we will evolve back, I do not know what to call it perhaps return, to the Void from which we all came (to Pure BEing devoid of consciousness). But I do know that balancing the thought forms experienced in human form helps us to move out of the experience of earth life. Of that, I am quite sure.

Vestiges of Old World Aspects Devolve

The last vestiges of the old world in which humanity has come to know and live unquestionably now take their leave amid the silence caused by chaos. The chaos erupting on planet earth shall continue for some time. And yet, this issue of the virus within one's self (the small egotistic self) changes from an outside infectious influence to one within. As all of humanity focuses on the silence within, the last vestiges of control by outside influences take their leave bit by bit, little by little until at last full sovereignty, full freedom of the soul is achieved. Again as noted previously, not all souls have chosen to tap into and awaken to the truth held within them.

As the world continues to evolve and devolve older aspects, we, the White Winged Consciousness of Nine, are ready and waiting to assist those not yet ready to let go of the separation held within their own selves. For it is only when one unquestionably seeks nothing outside one's Self (the Higher Self accessible through silence) that the states of consciousness, awareness of other levels of BEingness arrive bit by bit, little by little.

We as part of that true awakening of Self, are a group consciousness having seemed to live, as you, in physical form upon the planet earth as single humans. And having achieved that full sovereignty are now grouped, coalesced, if you will, as one group of consciousness, united in effort and purpose of spreading the Love and Light of Oneness.

As each human moves through the process of awakening, there are many aspects, states of awareness to shift through. Each state of awareness spirals, so to speak, to an increased state of awareness. Know that as each individual human's awareness increases, the chaos may appear to increase as well until one reaches a certain point in its own consciousness where it is no longer distracted by outside infectious influence but guided thoroughly, daily, moment by moment by its own Higher Self.

SamIAMproductions.com

Wag The Dog: Infectious Influence

"Things are getting dicey" (a word I do not normally hear nor use), I hear, as many people continue to search for toilet paper and other necessities while preparing for greater restrictions than the current government mandated two-week stay at home order.

We are living in a time when the infectious influence of thought waves is at its peak. We have the opportunity to choose, once again, love or fear. It is with this choice, this reaction, this emotion that that choice is made. All now hold within themselves the very power they have chosen to give away by believing in a power outside them. It is only through tapping into the higher aspects of ones Self that one learns the truth.

All on earth is illusion, and yet as one appears to be within the earth, within the illusion, one must follow ones own discernment and resonance. Those resonating with the fear of infectious influence that now overpowers the earth choose a path of experience much differently than those choosing to experience the love and the power within. As this global catastrophe continues to unfold on unprecedented levels, it is in the best interest of ones self to silently tap into this inner source of wisdom. For it is only through tapping into ones inner source of wisdom that one remains calm within the storm.

Author's Experiences

Tapping into higher states of consciousness begins with 4D, a rather risky realm to tap into due to various characteristics, so one must achieve and maintain a higher vibrational rate to avoid attracting what may be referred to as 'negative, non-helpful influences'. Veils of illusion are thinning so it is becoming easier to tap into this emotional astral realm. Those tapping into what is thought of as the 4D realm of illusion receive intel, so to speak, from 4D aspects of consciousness. And yet, we must each follow our own truth. We must each feel and sense what it is as a soul we have chosen to experience. Those that have chosen to experience power beyond belief, love beyond fear, now come forward to gather with like minds and pave the way to the New Earth for those choosing otherwise.

It is with the greatest respect, that as a human being, I choose fear to no longer lead my way. I choose love to experience greater and greater aspects of BEing.

SAM

Wayshowers, Come Forth

"The world spins totally out of control as the elite make their final last moves to harvest as many souls to continue the game of limitation, control and enslavement. Know that as these things occur, which are meant to secure this harvest to the fullest extent, many will not fall prey to these feeble attempts, for it is time, finally, in your world, for the greatest awakening of all time and space. Planet earth has securely been enmeshed within the throes of forgetfulness, forgetting the true state of its origins.

"We, the White Winged Consciousness of Nine trust that those now awakening and fully awakened will assist many (people) lying on the cusp of forgetfulness. It is time, dear ones, to come forth to assist your sisters and brothers of Light that have forgotten who they really are. This is the time of the Great Awakening for all upon planet earth, and yet this time will prolong to its maximum extent as long as many unawakened souls allow themselves to fall prey to the manipulations of what many refer, to themselves, the elite. Know that as the consciousness of humanity rises to its greatest extent in all the history of the world, higher realm forces, if you will, are available to assure that the elite, as they refer to themselves, will not be as successful in their attempts for greed and control as they had wished.

"It is with the greatest respect that we now ask those sitting behind the sidelines to come forward to assist as many (people) possible in this Great Awakening of True Self. One need not fall prey to the manipulation of these consciousnesses but to merely pay attention to what is in ones own field of consciousness, for each individual now faces its own inner demons as what appears as the manipulations of elite forces seem to control the globe.

"It is not, nor has it ever been, wise to continually force one's beliefs upon another. And so, before taking our leave, for this message, we ask all to consider what appears as the consciousness outside one's self when addressing others on this subject matter. Yes, those not understanding not yet ready to awaken will remain with closed minds, hearts, eyes and ears to all efforts to save themselves from the greed and control of what appear as elite forces. Know that as each soul takes this time to experience the balancing of expressions upon earth, many have not chosen to awaken to the truth of True BEing. Those of earth who are now awakened, stay clear of those appearing to be totally asleep. Assist only, when approached, those wishing to understand the sense of something more beyond what is seen and heard by human senses.

Yonder Classes

In the midst of a government shut-in, some people are now using video conferencing software, which I am leery of using due to my seeming karmic experience as using it to gather private data and control the masses during the Atlantean Age. Having researched owner data for the most popular free software used, it only confirms my choice to avoid this type of software to conduct bi-monthly classes. And so upon waking I am well aware of inviting certain previous class attendees to a class conducted on the ethereal realm of consciousness.

During class, I led the small group through a mind experiment where we check our three prominent bodies: the physical, astral and ethereal. Class excerpts are below.

Physical Body: Be aware of aches and pains as clues to the body's changing DNA, for we are once again taking on the 12 strands of DNA used to experience earth life aeons ago. This does cause aches and pains (imagine, if you will, living in a body that is dying but at the same time rejuvenating). Assuring that the body is flushed with good water (spring water, bottled at the source is best as it contains the live energy of Mother Gaia) assists the process.

Astral Body: Envision your astral body (1st auric field, as known by some people) and check for tears or weak areas, which are evident upon emotional reactions. Clear all judgment; recognize the human's true state as souls here to experience and express and remain in a state of neutrality to avoid negative attractions.

Ethereal Body: Continue to fill your ethereal body (known as the 2nd auric field beyond the astral field by some people) with Love and Light, remain in your own field of consciousness and be continuously open to guidance from your own Higher Self.

Class concluded with a round of three vocalized OMs.

SAM

Zoning Into 5D Consciousness

Life continues to amaze and delight as I follow what many refer to as higher intuition. Today the thought of leaving behind the fear mongering state now held by many to go take money out of the bank repeated, while under what appears as world-wide government restrictions, until I finally gave in and left the house. Wondering if my parking spot would be open upon my return, birds singing greeted me as I drove to and from the bank to make my quick ATM transaction. Families strolled down streets as people riding bicycles rode by. It seemed like a much different world, more filled with love and joy than ever before in my short human history of nearly seventy years.

And as usual, upon finding my parking spot open (a small miracle here where there are no assigned spots and everyone fights to park in the small lot outside my second-story window), and walking towards the front door of my building the thought of walking to the water's edge controlled both legs. What a lovely day to once again sit overlooking the very wide expanse of water to bridge both lower and upper worlds with mine, bringing in and grounding the Light of One!

Upon finishing my joy-filled task I again headed for the door of my building, amazed while watching violet light stream from the sun to cleanse earth. And once again, intuition guided me to check my mailbox, for only the third time in the three years I've lived here. You see, living

Author's Experiences

within a fairly constant state of 5D has led to many diversions from 3D reality. The need to waft through piles of daily advertisements and unnecessary mail is one of those elements that I have found a way to avoid, by paying for and forwarding all mail to a post office box miles away. Oddly, the mail system will not forward junk mail nor does the post office fill boxes with junk mail! So imagine my surprise when I opened the unused mail box steps from my door to find mail addressed to neighbors and a key to obtain larger mail. Imagine the surprise of someone who waited weeks to find out what happened to the love-filled gift sent from an adult child to their ailing parent. I was fortunate enough to deliver that unopened gift after removing it from its perch.

One may wonder no more about what it is like to live in a 5D state of consciousness for this is what it's all about, listening to and following that subtle guidance from one's Higher Self. And when we do miracles become ordinary occurrences!

SAM

About The Author

SAM, author of the "Lightworker's Log Book Series," is a minister (ordained by Sanctuary of the Beloved Church Priesthood and Order of Melchizedek), channel of higher realms, metaphysical teacher, founder of SAM I AM PROductions (**SamIAMproductions.com**) and administrator of the popular Internet resource, Lightworker's Log. Spreading Spirit's message of Oneness throughout the globe, SAM is a wayshower helping humanity to learn the truth of BEing so humanity can return all unique figments back to *All That Is.*

The Lightworker's Log Book Series

Book One: Death of the Sun
Book Two: A Change in Perception
Lightworker's Log :-) Transformation
Manifesting: Lightworker's Log
Prayer Treatments: Lightworker's Log
Adventures in Greece and Turkey
Earth Angels
Return to Light: John of God Helps
Bits of Wisdom
Book of One :-) Volume 1
Book of One :-) Volume 2
Book of One :-) Volume 3
Book of One :-) Volume 4
Book of One :-) Volume 5
After Death, Communications...WOW!

INDEX

2
2012 · 86, 92, 93

3
3D · 44, 76, 87, 129, See dimensions
3D reality · See 3D

4
4D · 123, See dimensions

5
5D · 128
5D Earth · See New Earth

A
A Course in Miracles · 83
A Mass Of Consciousness That Has Not Experienced Life In Human Form Nor As Souls · 80
aberrant energy · See energy
aches and pains · 126
adamantine · 69
agreements · 75
aliens · 109
All That Is · *10, 9, 17, 18, 26, 48, 58, 65, 66, 106, 118, 130*
Ascended Masters · 99
Ascension Process · 15, 21, 31, See ascension
asleep · 125
Aspects of Higher Self · 51
Aspects of My Higher Self · 83, 101, 106, 115
aspects of the small self · 3, 96
Astral Body · 126
astral energies · 20
astral realm · 123
Atlantean Age · 126
Atlanteans · 32
auric field · 126
awaken · xiii, 5, 6, 13, 24, 48, 60, 69, 77, 117
awakened · 124
awakening · xiii, 5, 21, 24, 55, 67, 79, 116
awareness · 5, 22, 27, 34, 35, 36, 38, 39, 44, 50, 59, 65, 66, 76, 78, 79, 80, 84, 85, 112

B
balance · xiii, 12, 28, 68, 101, 119
bands of consciousness · See consciousness
BEing · xiii, 8, 10, 11, 18, 21, 24, 32, 33, 34, 35, 38, 41, 48, 60, 75, 77, 78, 99, 100, 106, 112, 116, 119, 130
BEing of One · *100*
BEingness · 8, 28, 38, 55, 65, 96, 112
beliefs · xiii, 20, 66, 79, 83, 88, 93, 101, 106
belongings · 88
Bible · *92*
body aches · *104*
body changes · 32
body heat · *104, 105*
body/mind system · *9*
brain altered · 109

Index

C

carbon-based · 21, 32
catastrophes · 32, 33, 69
catastrophic events · 45
celestial beings · 9
Change · 5, 130
channel · 20, 23, 43, 65, 80, 96, 98, 99, 118, 130
chaos · 10, 11, 12, 13, 18, 24, 28, 30, 35, 36, 38, 40, 46, 53, 54, 55, 58, 69, 76, 81, 82, 105, 106, 108, 120
chaotic · 7, 49, 81, 82
chaotic action · See chaotic
chaotic event · See chaos
Christ Consciousness · 69, 77, 104, 105, 111
classes · 126
cleansing · 3, 15, 33, 50, 51, 103, 114
clues · *xiii, 79, 102*
collective thought · See mass consciousness
compassion · *9*
confusion · 10, 11, 35
Conglomeration Of Higher Realm Aspects · 41
conscious response · 13
consciousness · xiii, 5, 7, 8, 10, 11, 12, 13, 14, 18, 19, 24, 27, 31, 33, 38, 39, 42, 43, 44, 46, 49, 53, 54, 57, 59, 60, 61, 65, 66, 67, 68, 69, 71, 76, 77, 78, 80, 81, 82, 83, 84, 85, 96, 99, 104, 107, 114, 117, 119
Consciousness · 7, 8, 9, 10, 11, 5, 9, 17, 23, 24, 28, 29, 33, 35, 42, 44, 49, 51, 53, 58, 60, 66, 69, 75, 77, 84, 85, 102, 104, 105, 112, 115
control · 30, 82, 89, 108, 120, 124, 125, 126
Creation · 14
Creator · 20, 55
crystalline · 3, 5, 15, 32
cure · 109

cycle of time on earth · 86

D

dark night of the soul · 91
Death · 6, 32, 130
Dennis William Hauck · 89
dense matter · 71
dimensional realms · 17
dimensions · 75, 79, 112, See dimensional
Dimensions Of Consciousness · 78
discordant energies · 26
dissolving the current personality · 89, 95
Divine One · 31
Divine Spark · 69
DNA · *26, 104*, 126
downloads · 15, 113
dream · 48, 75, 76, See dreams
dreams · 52, 87, 88
dreamtime · See dreams
duality · 3, 6, 9, 40, 60, 84, 114, 115

E

earth · 120, 124
earth plane · 12
earth's magnetics · 22
eating habits · 118
ego · 8, 71, 81, 82, 89, 90, 91, 101
egotic · 73, 83
egotistic self · 120
elite · 124
emotion · 4, 5, 9, 18, 67, 82
emotions · 5, 6, 10, 33, 89, 91, 111
energetic frequencies · See frequency
energies · 9, 15, 17, 22, 25, 30, 36, 50, 58, 65, 75, 80, 98, 99, 111, See energy

Index

energy · 20, 33, 49, 86, 91, 92, 98, 100, 112, 113, 114
energy field · 113, See energy
Essence · 28, 65, 116
ethereal · 37, 65, 79, 112
Ethereal Body · 127
ethereal realm · 126
evolution · 7, 14, 24, 42, 46, 53, 99
exhaustion · See naps
experience and expression · 13, 23, 50, 80, 85, 105, 111

F

faith · 7, 58
family · 71, 75, 79, 81, 82, 87, 88, 93, 94, 99, 118
family life · 79
family members · 82, See family
family trip · See family
family turmoil · 99, See family
fear · 6, 18, 24, 68, 99, 122
fearful · See fear
field of consciousness · 27, 49, 66, 81
financial needs · 80
financial system · 108
flu · *104*
fluey feeling · See flu
foods · 15
formless states · 7, 46, 51
formlessness · 10
free will · 19, 105, 116
freedom · 13, 22, 23, 24, 80, 86, 89, 94
Freedom codes · 22
Freedom Codes · 6, 22
freedom of the soul · 120
frequency · 20, 38, 50, 104, 105, 111, 116, 118, 119
Frequency · 20
full moon · 30
future · 4, 33, 78

G

Gaia · See Mother Earth
Galactic Federation · 5, 3, 46, 108, 110
game · xiii, 5, 6, 12, 13, 22, 32, 33, 42, 44, 46, 56, 59, 71, 73, 83, 84, 85, 101, 107
Garden of Eden · 118
gas · 78
gatekeepers · 45
ginger · 70
global catastrophe · 122
God · 26, 130
Goddess Of Wisdom · 8, 10, 98, 99
Golden Age · 15, 48, 55, 56, 119
Golden Age of Oneness and Truth · 48
government · 126
grace and ease · 40, 50
grand event · 35
Great Awakening · 96, 124
Great Awakening of True Self · 125
Great Central Sun · 6, 25, 66
greater purpose · 86
greed · 125
greed and control · 5
grid · 45
Gridkeepers · 45
grounding · 128
group Consciousness · 23
Group Consciousness of Aspects of *All That Is* · 66
group of souls · 6
Guidelines · 6, 34

H

habits · 42, 89, 90
harvest · 124
headache · 80
headaches · 104
health · 15
heart based · 12

Index

Heart Opening · 9, *102*
heart pain · See Heart Opening
heart resonance · 12
heart singing · See Heart Opening
heart's core · 11, 56
heart's wisdom · 50
higher aspects of Self · 10
higher consciousness · 90, 91
higher realms · 10, 7, 20, 23, 27, 40, 75, 99, 130
Higher Realms Of Consciousness · 10
Higher Self · 40, 111, 120, 127, 129
higher vibrational level · 15
holographic · 7, 22
Holographic Reality · 5, 7
home-base less · 86
human form · 5, 6, 12, 13, 26, 28, 34, 35, 49, 73, 76, 79, 80, 84, 102, 105, 118, 119
human senses · 125
humanity · 5, 6, 7, 8, 9, 10, 17, 18, 21, 22, 24, 26, 27, 32, 34, 35, 36, 40, 41, 42, 45, 48, 51, 55, 56, 58, 59, 60, 65, 68, 71, 76, 98, 100, 105, 106, 114, 117, 130
humans · 5, 7, 9, 13, 17, 25, 27, 28, 32, 33, 35, 36, 38, 42, 65, 69, 71, 79, 105, 119
hydration · 15

I

I AM Presence · 6, 10, 26
illusion · 8, 9, 12, 13, 17, 22, 23, 39, 44, 46, 47, 48, 49, 50, 59, 60, 61, 69, 72, 76, 81, 82, 84, 85, 86, 93, 96, 100, 101, 106, 115, 116, 117, 118, 119
infectious influence · 120, 122
inner demons · 125
intestinal distress · 112, See rough night
intuition · 90, 91, 93, 128
intuitive insight · See intuition

J

Journaling · 86

K

knowledge · 26, 50, 77, 105

L

Law of Attraction · 13, 14, 84, 119
Law Of One · 18, 31, 34, 71
Lemuria · 33
Lemurian Council of Twelve · 10, 15, 16, 21, 22, 23, 30, 31, 34, 39, 45, 48, 71, 72, 84, 96, 116, 118
Lemurians · 32
lifestyle · 15
Lifestyle · 5, 15
Light · 7, 9, xiii, 7, 9, 18, 32, 33, 34, 36, 45, 48, 58, 59, 60, 71, 103, 114, 130
light and darkness · 97
light codes · *104*
Light of One · 7, 9, 34, 45, 48
Light Of Truth · 48
lightbody · 32
lightworker · 45
linear reality · 7
lost souls · See soul
love · 122
Love · 9, 6, 7, 8, 18, 31, 36, 59, 60, 68, 103, 114, 115, 117
LOVE · See Oneness
Love and Light of Oneness · 121
lower self · 10

M

magnetic field · 22
manipulation · 125

134

Index

mass confusion · 58, See confusion
mass consciousness · 108
mass human death · 33
massive change · 7, 46
matrix · 12, 17, 22, 23, 60, 66, 81, 82, 106
Mayans · 32
maze · 44, 48, 66, 73, 81, 98, 111, See illusion
media · 24, 67
meditating · 67, See meditation
meditation · 10, 68, 85, 90
mind/body/spirit complex · 41
mind/body/spirit system · xiii
Mirrors · 6, 31, 38, 39
misthoughts · 31, 46, 106, See thought Forms
Monad · 6, 28
Monads · See Higher Self
morph · 3, 89, 95, 111
morphing · 6, 32, 33, See morph
Mother Earth · 32
Mother Nature · 87
Mother Void · See Void
moving · 12, 13, 18, 20, 27, 31, 44, 48, 65, 66, 80, 88, 96, 102, 107, 117
multidimensional · 34
multidimensional experiences · 110
Multi-Generational Beliefs · 9, 106
my consciousness · 86

N

nap · 80
naps · See nap
negative aspects · 3
negative thought forms · 36
neutrality · 67, 127
New 5D Earth · 36, See New Earth
New Earth · 6, 22, 23, 30, 32, 35, 36, 45, 58, 112, 123, See 5D Earth

New World · See New Earth
Nirvana · 11, 53, 105
Non-judgment · 60
non-local reality · 7, 34
No-Thing · *101*

O

Old World · 120
One · 7, 8, 9, 12, 14, 17, 27, 28, 35, 36, 45, 48, 53, 55, 58, 59, 60, 69, 71, 75, 97, 101, 104, 130
One BEing Of Light · *102*
Oneness · 5, 6, 7, 3, 6, 7, 8, 9, 10, 17, 18, 23, 28, 30, 31, 35, 36, 37, 39, 40, 48, 53, 55, 56, 58, 60, 68, 71, 76, 84, 87, 92, 94, 96, 100, 101, 111, 114, 116, 117, 118, 119, 130
Oneness is held by all · 53

P

past incarnation · 98
path of evolution · 14
Physical Body · 126
physical form · 28, 33, 34, 40, 46, 53, 54, 71, 84, 98, 106, 111
physical forms · 5
planet · 19, 24, 29, 31, 32, 46, 48, 55, 60, 71, 111, See Mother Earth
planetary changes · 32
Pleiadian Council of Twelve · 10, 25
Pleiadians · 10, 57, 65, 103
ploys · 6, 24
portal · 31, 38
possessions · 88, 89, 92, 93
POWER · 9
prescriptions · 92
Presence · 26, 91
Present Moment · 7, 60
Primordial Awareness · *85*

135

Index

processing · 28, 51
Purging · 10

R

Radiate love · 83
rain · 114
reactions · 55
Reality · 6, 11, 28, 34, 58, 68, 115
rebirth · 22, 73
relationships · 16
remaining neutral · 60
rough night · 112, 118
runny nose · See rough night

S

safety · 11
SAM · 11, 32, 33, 52, 67, 68, 86, 111, 122, 126, 128, 130
seeding of humanity · 35
Self · 6, 5, 10, 15, 18, 21, 22, 23, 26, 27, 28, 30, 34, 35, 50, 54, 55, 56, 59, 66, 77, 84, 85, 100, 103
Self of I AM · 92
separation · 5, 9, 10, 18, 24, 27, 29, 30, 35, 36, 37, 38, 39, 40, 46, 56, 60, 61, 77, 80, 81, 82, 83, 84, 93, 96, 97, 114, 117, 118
shortages · 108
signs of change · 88
simultaneous experience · 46
Sisters and Brothers of Light · 8, 18, 19, 60, 96
sixth sense · 5
sleeping habits · *104*
small mind of one · 29, 77, 79, 87, 91, 96
soul · 7, xiii, 5, 12, 13, 15, 18, 22, 23, 32, 42, 43, 45, 46, 47, 49, 51, 52, 53, 56, 69, 71, 73, 76, 81, 84, 85, 86, 90, 97, 98, 99, 100, 101, 102, 105, 111
soul choice · 7, 19, 44
soul experience · 122
soul plan · 7, 19, 42, 52, 110
Soul Self · 7, 59
souls · 16, 23, 24, 31, 33, 37, 38, 43, 44, 46, 48, 56, 60, 61, 65, 67, 69, 76, 77, 82, 84, 104
Source · 10, 13, 20, 48, 61, 100, 102
sovereign · 23, 77
sovereignty · 31, 120
spiritual awareness · 35
spiritual transformation · 90
Sri Nisargadatta Maharaj · 85
star · 29, 46
starseeds · 45
subsequent cold · 105
sun · 17, 65, 112
survival · 10, 11

T

temperature · 20
The Emerald Tablet: Alchemy for Personal Transformation · *See* Dennis William Hauck
The Matrix · 100
Theosophical Society · 99, 109
Thought · 5, 6, 9, 5, 35, 85, 116
thought forms · xiii, 12, 13, 14, 17, 28, 35, 36, 37, 46, 75, 78, 79, 84, 85, 112, 114, 116, 117, 118, 119
thoughts · 6, 10, 12, 33, 36, 42, 48, 58, 67, 68, 81, 106, 111, 114
time/space continuum · 3, 7, 16, 38, 46, 50, 69, 71, 103
timeline · 5, 6, 18, 31, 57
timelines · 5, 18, 31
tornado · 87
traditions · 87
True BEing · 125
True Self · 28, See Self

Index

Truth · *7, 9, 17, 31, 34, 35, 36, 40, 48, 60, 114, 115*

U

Ultimate Reality · 44
United States · 24
unity · 3, 14, 40, 68, 80
Unity Consciousness · 28, 29
Unity of Oneness · 80
unseen realms · 9, 102
urinate · See rough night

V

Veils of illusion · 123
vestiges · 120
vibration · 38, 44, 61, 76, 112
vibrational range · 66
vibrational rate · 27, 34, 68, 123
vibrational state · 46, *See* vibration
virus · 108, 120

visioning · 86
Void · 7, 33, 60, 96, 101, 117, 119

W

Wag The Dog · 122
water · 126
watery eyes · See rough night
Wayshower · 45, 124, 130
Wayshowers · 31
wheel of life · 97
White Winged Consciousness of Nine · 11, 6, 9, 14, 17, 20, 24, 29, 35, 42, 44, 49, 53, 55, 58, 69, 75, 77, 84, 102, 105, 112, 120, 124
Whole · 19, 34, 35, 78, 82, 116, 118
Whole of BEingness · 38
Wholeness · 34, 38, 39, 55, 107, 118
WOW · 73, 95

www.ingramcontent.com/pod-product-compliance
Lightning Source LLC
LaVergne TN
LVHW041337080426
835512LV00006B/495